W9-CXZ-068

T-BIRDS

T-BIRDS

Doug Mitchel

MetroBooks

MetroBooks

An Imprint of Friedman/Fairfax Publishers

©1999 by Michael Friedman Publishing Group, Inc.

All rights reserved. No part of this publication may be reproduced,
stored in a retrieval system, or transmitted, in any form or by any
means, electronic, mechanical, photocopying, recording, or otherwise,
without prior written permission from the publisher.

Library of Congress Cataloging-in-Publication Data available upon request

ISBN 1-56799-753-8

Editor: Ann Kirby
Art Director: Jeff Batzli
Designer: Eddy Herch
Photography Editor: Valerie E. Kennedy
Production Manager: Camille Lee

Color separations by Ocean Graphics International Company Ltd
Printed in China by Leefung-Asco Printers Ltd.

10 9 8 7 6 5 4 3 2 1

For bulk purchases and special sales, please contact:
Friedman/Fairfax Publishers
Attention: Sales Department
15 West 26th Street
New York, NY 10010
212/685-6610 FAX 212/685-1307

Visit our website:
http://www.metrobooks.com

PAGE 2: The 1957 Thunderbird was the last of the two-seat T-Birds (until at least the year 2000).
Its sleek, well-proportioned fins and distinctive egg-crate grille are classics of 1950s style.

PAGE 5: Beneath the hooded dash of the 1957 Thunderbird, touches of turned metal echoed details in some
of Ford's full-size cars, creating an aesthetic theme that connected many of the cars in Ford's lineup.

PAGE 7: The 1973 Sports Roadster featured a removable fiberglass tonneau cover,
which gave the four-passenger Bullet Bird the sleek look of a two-seater.

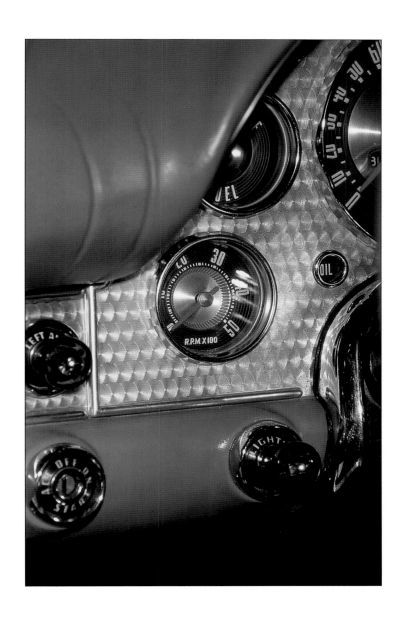

Contents

INTRODUCTION

When Ford rolled out the all-new Thunderbird in 1954, they could not have predicted the popularity of their latest creation. Sure, their marketing people had told them that the market was ripe for a speedy American roadster that would look as good cruising the boulevard as it did dragging down on the strip. But could they have known that this little two-seater would evolve into an American icon, a legendary marque that would soldier on for more than four decades?

Every car maker dreams of building a best-seller, but designing an American icon is not something that can be done in any boardroom. From its inception, the sleek Thunderbird captured the hearts of the car-driving public. The crisp and classic body lines were accented by a sporty feel, providing drivers with a capable form of transportation. The first few years saw improvements being added that only increased demand for the sexy roadster, and the car was successfully reshaped and remarketed several times through the 1960s.

Yet the Bird saw dark times, too. The bulk of the automotive industry fell into a design slump in the mid-1970s, and with fuel economy beginning to weigh heavily on everyone's mind, cars became less about fun and more about utility. The Thunderbird was not immune to the trend. Frumpy shapes melded with an excess of bland accessories, and the Bird soon began to look just like many of the other failures on the market.

But despite the poor aesthetic and the resulting lack of sales, the Thunderbird remained a popular nameplate. The car-buying audience had changed, and some of this new wave actually preferred the latest iteration. In fact, as today's nostalgia-obsessed consumers look back on the cars of their youth, it is not the classic chromed and finned Bird of the late-1950s that rings a bell, but the boxy, masculine lines of the mid-1970s Birds that bring nostalgic tears to their eyes.

During the 1980s the Thunderbird rose from the ashes and again set a trend in American automotive design. The 1984 Thunderbird, criticized by some as being too rounded and nebulous, proved to be one of the most influential designs in recent history. Streamlined and curvy, its new bodywork complemented by added performance, the '84 Bird was a sign of things to come, a precursor to the wildly successful Taurus. Not only were the new cars more powerful than the models they replaced, they delivered a more potent punch while staying efficient. Technology was finally looking like a friend.

BELOW: Three little Thunderbirds, all in a row: the first-generation Birds were the epitome of cool in the 1950s.

Regardless of how powerful and beautiful the mid-1980s Thunderbird was, it was no match for the foreign competition flooding the American car market. Japanese imports had been coming ashore for more than a decade, usually in one of two flavors: bargain-basement economy cars or expensive luxury models. But the new cars coming from Japan in the 1980s were different. Attractive, reliable, and economical, cars from companies like Honda, Toyota, and Nissan had a profound impact on the American market. Consumers found themselves wanting a better car for less money, and they were willing to look beyond Detroit to find it.

It was the beginning of the end for the aging Thunderbird. By the time the 1990s rolled around, the Bird was getting a little long in the tooth. The fact that the Thunderbird was sleeker and more powerful than ever did little to hide the fact that it also was crippled with an outdated drivetrain. Rear wheel drive was now a thing of the past in all but the upper level of the luxury car segment. Ford needed to either rethink the Thunderbird from the ground up, or put it on the shelf.

ABOVE: In the mid-eighties, the Thunderbird shook up the car market once again with a groundbreaking aerodynamic design.

In 1997, after forty-two years of ups and downs, Ford announced that the aging Thunderbird would be laid to rest. But Thunderbird enthusiasts, loyal to the very end, refused to believe their beloved car was gone forever. Despite Ford's insistence that the Bird was permanently grounded, rumors of an all-new model for the upcoming millennium began to circulate among car enthusiasts within days of the company's announcement of the T-Bird's demise.

And it turns out that the rumors were correct. Ford unveiled plans for a brand-new Thunderbird for the year 2000 at the Detroit Auto Show in January 1998. And the reaction from the automotive press—as well as from Thunderbird loyalists—has been phenomenal. Following on the success of the retrostyled Mustang—as well as Volkswagen's New Beetle and Mazda's trailblazing Miata—the new Bird is modeled on the classic lines of the 1955–57 roadster. The challenge for Ford, of course, has been to marry that fun-fun-fun styling with the safety and emissions requirements of the modern age, and at a non-prohibitive cost. But Ford's designers have risen to such challenges before, and it seems certain that like the mythological bird for which it was named, the Thunderbird will rule the skies—or at least the roads—once more.

CHAPTER ONE

THE EARLY BIRD

W hen World War II ended—and along with it the years of rationing everything from nylon to steel—Americans found themselves hungry for nearly everything they had sacrificed during the long battle overseas.

The vast majority of the population had gone without common necessities as well as more luxurious items, and with their victorious soldiers back at home and the economy booming, they were ready, willing, and able to purchase almost anything that appeared.

Automotive designs of the immediate postwar era lacked not only style but also speed and spirit, and people wanted more. Automotive designers in Detroit were intrigued with the European vehicles that were beginning to appear in the United States, and many autocrafters began noodling with concepts of their own. By the early 1950s, several offerings from competing American manufacturers spurred Ford into action.

1954–1957: The Birth of the Bird

BY THE TIME THESE SPORTY new imports raised the eyebrows of Ford brass, two members of the company's design staff, Franklin Q. Hershey and William P. Boyer, had already been tinkering with the idea of a new roadster

for Ford. Impressed by the competitive offerings that were beginning to appear on streets and racetracks across the United States, the pair began to put their own versions on paper in the early 1950s. Hershey and Boyer felt that consumers, tired of the bulbous, utilitarian styles on the showroom floors, were seeking a car that reflected the fun, excitement, and optimism of the times: it was a good time to be an American, and Americans were craving a

PAGES 10–11: The 1957 Bird was sleek and stylish, with well-proportioned fins at the back end and a brilliant chrome grille up front. It is the most sought after of all the classic T-Bird models. ABOVE: The 1955 debuted in February 1954 as a wooden mock-up, and consumers were happily surprised that the real car, which rolled off assembly lines in September that same year, didn't stray very far from the exciting prototype.

A Timeless Car, an Immortal Name

O n February 20, 1954, Ford presented the car that would mark the company's entry into the sports car market at the Detroit Auto Show. Yet the stylish little roadster that debuted as a wooden mock-up very nearly did so without a name. In a frenzy to find just the right moniker to apply to their new baby, Ford decided to hold an in-house contest, inviting each member of the design team to suggest a name for their latest creation. The winner, Alden "Gib" Giberson, chose a legendary name for a car that was destined to become a legend. The Thunderbird pervades the

mythology of many Native American tribes. It is a supernatural bird that produces thunder by the heat of its wings, and flashes lightning from its mouth or eyes—among many tribes, it is the ruler of the sky. The name and all that it implied perfectly captured Ford's vision for the new car. Ford announced the new name just one day before the car's premiere, on February 19. Giberson won the prize—a new suit and two pairs of pants—and got to design the first Thunderbird emblem, a bird with wings spread, appropriately cast in silver and turquoise.

good-time American car. Responding to this pent-up desire, Ford general manager Lewis D. Crusoe gave his designers the green light for a swoopy new design.

Aiming for a car that combined the style and flair of a sports car with the comfort of a boulevard cruiser, Ford wanted to produce a car that was at once powerful and smooth and that would offer competent handling while retaining a high level of comfort. Thus, Hershey and Boyer had a captive audience for their thoughts on how Ford could get its feet wet in the sports car market.

Meanwhile, Chevrolet's Corvette went on sale as a 1953 model. Geared toward the true sports car crowd, it was draped in sensual bodywork and rode on a performance-tuned chassis and power train. This was a radical departure from the usual American offerings, and it proved to be the final impetus Ford needed to bring its own two-seater to the market. The Corvette had sparked the nation's interest in European-inspired sports cars, but it lacked simple features to which American drivers were accustomed, like roll-down windows. By providing these amenities, Ford carved a comfortable niche in the newly identified market.

BELOW: The two-seater Thunderbird lasted for only three years but, with more power and luxury, it outsold its closest competitor, Chevy's sporty but somewhat crude Corvette.

The new Ford Thunderbird made its initial appearance at the Detroit Auto Show in early 1954. Many believed that this glamorous new creation, almost a year away from production, would prove to be merely a show car with little relation to what would wind up being sold to the public as a production car. These doubters were proven quite wrong.

1954–1955:
The Thunderbird Comes to Roost

THE 1955 THUNDERBIRD WENT INTO production on September 9, 1954, and the final product was a mirror

image of what showgoers had seen. Despite being the last entry in the two-seater market, the all-new Thunderbird was greeted with open arms and sold wildly.

The Corvette may have primed the market for the T-Bird, but Ford's designers had the inspiration for their exciting new car long before the Corvette hit the road. And the two cars were as different as day and night. The focus of the Thunderbird had been different from the start—a smoother, more glamorous silhouette, a more luxurious interior, and a more powerful engine set the T-Bird apart from the crude and underpowered Corvette.

Unlike the Corvette, the Thunderbird featured side windows that actually rolled up and down, and the body panels were pressed steel rather than fiberglass. The new Thunderbird was more than 13 inches (33cm) shorter than any other model in the Ford catalog, and its trim size added to the sporty nature of the car. Power for the new Bird was delivered by a 292-cubic-inch V8 engine that produced 193 horsepower with a manual transmission. Five more ponies were on tap when the T-Bird was ordered with a Ford-O-Matic trans.

This combination of looks, functionality, and power sent the Thunderbird roaring through dealerships at breakneck speed. It eclipsed its main competitor, the Corvette (which was a mere V6), even though the Thunderbird cost some $200 more. In 1955, the first full year of sales for both the Bird and the Vette, the Corvette sold in numbers approaching 700 units, while the Thunderbird sold more than 16,000 units. America had fallen for the Thunderbird, and the love affair was only beginning.

1956:
Improving the Breed

ALTHOUGH THE DEBUT OF THE Thunderbird had gone very well, several changes were made to the 1956 models. One of the most obvious was the addition of the bumper-mounted Continental Kit at the tail end of the Bird. This adaptation allowed for more usable trunk space by mounting the spare tire outside, and it looked great,

ABOVE, LEFT: Richly appointed in contrasting-colored interior, this 1955 Bird is equipped with the under-dash air-conditioning unit.

ABOVE: There were quite a few improvements to the Thunderbird for 1956, including the glass vent windows up front and air vents on the side panels, both of which made for a more comfortable drive. LEFT: Two striking new options were available for the 1956 model. The continental kit mounted the spare tire on the back, freeing up trunk space and giving the Bird a distinguished look from the back. The removable hardtop was available with unique opera windows, which improved visibility and became a trademark feature of T-Bird design.

S P E C S

1955
Thunderbird
Coupe

Weight
2,837 lbs.
(1,058.2kg)

Engine type
V-8, 90 degree,
OHV

Engine displacement
292 ci

Horsepower
193

Transmission
Three-speed

Wheelbase
102 in. (259.08cm)

Overall length
175.3 in. (445.3cm)

Overall width
70.2 in. (178.3cm)

Overall height
52.2 in. (132.6cm)

Exterior colors
Five

Interior colors
Four

Options
Automatic transmission,
higher output V-8, (8)
tube radio with antenna,
MagicAire heater, wire
wheelcovers, tinted glass

Total production
16,155

even if it did change the handling quite a bit. A pair of glass vent windows was also added to benefit the driver and passenger on spirited drives, and small vents were placed in each front quarter panel. These panels could be opened to allow more fresh air to pass through the interior, helping to keep the occupants cool on warm days.

A more striking change was the availability of portholes found on the sides of the removable hardtop. This option allowed for a slight improvement in visibility and allowed onlookers to see the lucky driver and passenger of the latest Thunderbird; it became a T-Bird trademark.

Beneath the subtly improved body, some substantial upgrades had been implemented. In the standard 292-cubic-inch engine, horsepower was rated at 202. New for 1956 was the 312-cubic-inch power plant, which delivered 225 horsepower. Both options exhaled through a rerouted exhaust that terminated at the outer corners of the rear bumper.

About the only common criticism of the 1955 models was the harshness of the ride. By attempting to retain some sports car traits, the engineers had provided a stiffer suspension than the average consumer preferred. By popular demand, the 1956 Thunderbird rode on softer, four-leaf springs that provided the desired comfort level. Improvements in the balance of the T-Bird also delivered better handling, but it was still far removed from true sports car performance. Offering a softer ride than the Vette, with more power than other sedans, the Thunderbird became the compromise car, gracefully straddling the racing and cruising segments of the sports car market. Since the Thunderbird had never been intended to compete face-to-face with the Corvette, this market position suited Ford to a T.

With changes come cost, and the 1956 Thunderbird saw its price increased to $3,151. Sales fell below 16,000 units, but the Thunderbird was still in demand.

1957:
A Fresh Face

JUST THE SLIGHT DECLINE IN sales between the 1955 and 1956 models sent the Ford design teams scurrying back to their drawing boards. In stark contrast to today's lengthy product runs, Detroit automakers in the 1950s were often known to completely redesign a vehicle for just a single year of sales. The 1957 Thunderbird is considered by many to be the best Bird model ever produced. Numerous improvements made the '57 longer, lower, and even faster than its predecessors.

At the front end, the Bird sported a larger bumper and housed a pair of rectangular parking lights. The grille was also larger, providing the new motors with much-needed cooling capabilities. The front quarter panels were treated to newly shaped wheel openings, and a new script logo was located near the slanted louvers on the front fender.

The wheelbase of the latest model remained unchanged, but the body was lengthened and included all-new sheet metal out back. The additional 6 inches (15cm) in length created enough room to allow the spare tire to ride inside the trunk again, but many buyers added the aftermarket Continental Kit because they liked the way it looked. In between the racy fins of the '57 sat a higher deck lid, which also provided additional cargo space. A new bumper at the rear end featured openings that allowed the dual exhausts to exhale through the portals.

The hardtop also saw a change in the buyer's choice of portholes or a solid roof. Since the first appearance of the tiny side windows, they had become all the rage, and nearly 75 percent of those buying in 1957 decided to get their roofs with the openings. Ten different exterior colors were offered, and the hardtop could be ordered in either a matching or contrasting hue.

Inside the Thunderbird, only minor changes were made. The shape of the seats had been greatly improved,

OPPOSITE: A restyled grille, rear deck, and brand-new bumpers were part of the package for the 1957 Bird. With the addition of the rakish tailfins, it became the most beloved iteration of all time, quickly achieving cult status among collectors. PRECEDING PAGES: To the amazement of consumers and the automotive press, the first Thunderbirds really were everything that Ford promised they would be. The 1955 Bird forged an indelible mark in the minds of auto buffs everywhere.

and the dashboard was given a hooded section to house the main instrument cluster. New touches of turned metal echoed that of some of Ford's full-size cars, creating an aesthetic theme connecting members of the Ford family.

Several modifications were implemented beneath the 1957 model, even though the wheelbase had remained unchanged. The rear springs were comprised of five leaves each (a throwback to the '55 model) in lieu of the four-leaf components of 1956. The extra length of the 1957 model required some stiffening of the chassis, which was accomplished by changing the shape of one of the cross-members. All these alterations provided the Thunderbird with a higher level of stability at the rear end, a lack of which had haunted the Bird since its inception.

At all four corners, smaller, 14-inch (35.5cm) wheels were found. The wheel covers encompassed the entire steel rim, adding additional detail and sparkle. Behind the smaller wheels were even larger brakes, which came in handy when utilizing the new levels of horsepower on tap.

The standard engine options were joined by two high-performance variations. The E-model breathed through a matching set of four-barrel Holley carburetors and pumped out 270 horsepower. For the truly power-hungry, there was the potent F-model. Still using a 312-cubic-inch block, the F-Birds were force-fed via a supercharger. Not many cars prowling the streets could compete with the F-model's output of 300 horsepower. Only 208 examples of the F-model were built, and it remains one of the most coveted Birds.

Ford's efforts on the 1957 models paid off. More than 21,000 Thunderbirds were sold that year, which marked the final appearance of the svelte, two-seater T-Bird.

1958–1960: The Square Bird

AFTER ONLY A FEW YEARS, American consumers were losing their appetite for two-seater automobiles.

BELOW: Ford earned a reputation on the track as well as on the street with race-prepared cars like the Battlebird, which drove to a second-place finish (behind a Ferrari) in a 1957 race at Smyrna Beach. Stock models earned similar reputations on the NASCAR circuit.

Head-to-Head with the Vette

It's been said that part of the Thunderbird's success was due to the shortcomings of its closest competitor, the Chevy Corvette. Released a year before the Bird hit the market, the Corvette tested the waters for a sporty new roadster, only to be thrown out of the pool by Ford's later entry. In 1956, the automotive media was beginning to write up the eulogy for the sporty Vette, and Ford hoped to push the process along by beating the Corvette at the track as well as in the showrooms.

The Thunderbird made its way onto the track in the form of the race-bred Battlebird, which debuted in Daytona Beach in February 1957. A total of four Battlebirds were assembled, all wearing the general silhouette of the civilian models, but their running gear was a bird of another color. The first two Battlebirds were tagged with vehicle identification numbers ending in 265 and 266. While the 265 was fitted with a moderate amount of racing bits, 266 was a pure racing machine. Its 312-cubic-inch engine was fitted to a four-speed Jaguar transmission. Both the engine and chassis were altered for racing, and the result was a highly competent package. But even with successes at the track, the Thunderbird was unable to displace the Corvette completely. More than forty years later, the Vette is still running strong, while the Bird has been at least temporarily grounded. So although the Battlebird won some of the early battles, it seems that perhaps Corvette has won the war.

ABOVE: The T-Bird was completely redesigned in 1958, growing 24 inches in length to make room for seating for four adults. PAGES 20-21: The classic hardtop of 1957, in signature pink. The '57 was the best-selling T-bird yet: more than 21,000 were built.

The lack of practicality was most likely the biggest reason—America was in the midst of the postwar baby boom, and families raising children required more space than the first Thunderbirds could provide. The declining sales figures prompted Ford's management to set a new course for the T-Bird in 1958.

1958:
The Square Birds Arrive

FORD'S GOAL FOR '58 WAS to make the Thunderbird more family-friendly while retaining its sporty spirit. The company's designers made a complete redesign, scrapping just about everything from the chassis up. The 1958 models did not share a single inch of sheet metal with the 1957s, and the ground-up redesign produced a brand-new, more aggressive Bird. More than 2 feet (60cm) longer and riding on a wheelbase that exceeded that of the '57 by 11 inches (28cm), the '58 T-Bird was also 1,000 pounds (454kg) heavier than its predecessor.

Production of the 1958s began in January of that year, with only the two-door hardtop offered initially. Plans for a convertible version had been approved in May 1957, but

the implementation of the all-new and somewhat tricky technology slowed production—the unit-body construction proved difficult to get dialed in on the assembly lines. Even the hardtop was not available until several months after the balance of the Ford lineup appeared in dealers' showrooms.

When it finally rolled into showrooms, the new Bird was hardly recognizable. Its larger, more angular body quickly prompted the automotive press to dub it the Square Bird. The enlarged cabin could accommodate four adults, although the car remained a two-door in order to retain some degree of its roadster styling. The roomier interior boasted front bucket seats, the first ever seen on an American car, along with a new console that camouflaged the driveshaft tunnel. The low-slung interior made the tunnel seem inordinately high, but disguised by the full-length console—also the first on an American car—it lent an air of coziness to the much bigger Bird, as both driver and front-seat passenger found themselves seated in their own personal cockpit. This aspect combined with the sleek new dashboard to create a Bird that looked—at least from the inside—like it could take off for the skies any minute.

While the new Bird couldn't really fly, it got a new engine that packed enough power that it seemed to fly along the highway. In an effort to propel the larger mass of the new model, a more potent V8 engine was installed. Displacing 352 cubic inches, the Interceptor engine produced 300

horsepower and proved to be an adequate motivator. The bigger V8 breathed in through a single four-barrel carburetor and exhaled through a dual exhaust. Power was delivered through one of three available transmissions. The buying options were the manual, overdrive, and the latest Cruise-O-Matic, which was the automatic choice for many. All of this new power was slowed by 11-inch (28cm) duo-servo brakes at each wheel. The 1958 Thunderbird rode on coil springs in the rear, which was the only such application until the appearance of the 1967 models.

Ford took a risk with such a radical redesign of a fairly successful car, but it turned out to be a good gamble. History shows us that 1958 was one of the automotive industry's worst years ever for sales of new vehicles, and Ford's fresh iteration was late to the table, putting it at a competitive disadvantage. Yet this big, bad, square Bird was the only American car other than the Corvette to increase its sales from the previous year. The Thunderbird

was all-new, and people wanted more than Ford could produce. In 1958, 37,000 Thunderbirds were sold, and as production failed to meet demand for the new model, nearly one thousand eager buyers were forced to wait until the following year.

1959:
Small Changes for
Fast Sellers

WITH THE PUBLIC still clamoring for the '58 T-Bird, Ford saw little reason to make sweeping changes for the next model year. An enormous number of changes to other cars in the Ford lineup left a

ABOVE: The 1958 Birds were longer, wider, and heavier than their predecessors, and sported a bold new front clip that included four headlights. RIGHT: Only minor alterations were made on the 1959 Thunderbirds, many of which were merely cosmetic in nature, such as the dash of chrome on the side panel bullets.

minuscule engineering budget for the T-Bird, but people continued to flock to Ford's showrooms, seeking "new" Thunderbirds that were essentially warmed-over '58s.

The sheet metal went unchanged, but trim alterations were rampant. The front grille sported a series of horizontal bars, a treatment that was mirrored on the taillight surrounds. The rectangular trim pieces on the doors were supplanted by a set of chromed bullets, which helped to smooth out the visual lines of the boxy design.

An abundance of color choices remained in the order book, forcing the buyer of a 1959 model to choose from eighteen solid colors or the forty-one two-tone options displayed. In the convenience department, a fully automated convertible roof was made available later in the model year. The new design made the large soft-top far more user-friendly than the earlier example. The convertible Thunderbird sold for $3,979, which was only a few hundred dollars more than the hardtop model, which went for $3,696.

Beneath the mildly modified bodywork, there were several improvements. The suspension had returned to an all-leaf-spring layout, which assisted in providing a comfortable ride while delivering decent handling capabilities. In contrast to the mere rumor of a bigger motor, the 1959 was available with an optional 430-cubic-inch, 350-horsepower engine from the Lincoln. This more potent power plant really gave the Thunderbird wings, the kind of power that many potential buyers wanted. Regardless of which engine was ordered, a new radiator, fan, and cooling tank were installed to help keep things cool.

Storage capacity in the '59 trunk was 20 cubic feet (0.5 cu m), mostly due to the boxier design of the body and the fact that the new car was far larger than the original models.

The combination of these minor changes proved to be a potent package. Sales skyrocketed to more than 67,000. It appeared that the gamble of changing the svelte two-seater Bird to a more practical layout was paying off for Ford.

1960:
If It Ain't Broke,
Don't Fix It

THE RAGING SUCCESS OF THE latest Square Birds prompted the management of Ford to leave well enough alone. The 1960 T-Birds rolled off the assembly line with only minor modifications.

The grille was once again altered, and a similar treatment was found at the tail end. The 1960 models were, however, fitted with all-new triple taillights at each corner. This change is probably the easiest way to recognize a '60.

The chromed bullet trim on the doors was changed. The Thunderbird name was scripted in chrome and applied to both side panels in place of the previous trim. Three sets of vertical bars adorned the rear quarter panels, reminiscent of the 1958 side trim.

In its efforts to produce a car with higher value, Ford began including hardware on the standard equipment list that had previously been optional. The driver's inside mirror was upgraded to the latest polarized glass, providing better vision, especially after the sun had gone down, and an outside mirror was added to the standard package.

RIGHT AND BELOW: 1960 would be another year of only cosmetic changes, thanks to the success of the previous year's models. The new, manually operated sunroof was the first ever offered, and provided a taste of open-air motoring to the hardtop buyer.

Inside the cockpit, new upholstery options were offered. The four-cubicle arrangement was unchanged and remained a popular feature.

An industry first was the manually operated sunroof. Called the Gold Top option, it was available for an additional $212, but only about twenty-five hundred people took advantage of the latest in open-air technology. The roof panel was operated via a chromed lever that rotated within a circular housing and allowed fresh air and sunshine to flow through the rectangular opening with a twist of the crank.

Color options remained abundant for 1960 with nineteen solid choices, although only twenty-eight two-tone variations were available. Even with fewer two-tone choices available than in previous years, it was still hard to find two Thunderbirds on any lot with the same combination.

Motivation for the 1960 models remained the same as in 1959. The 300-horsepower, 352-cubic-inch engine could be upgraded to the 350-horsepower 430 for an extra $200. A new chrome dress-up kit for visible hardware was also offered to those who liked their go to have some extra show.

Prices for the 1960 Birds had climbed slightly; the hardtop listed for $3,755, with the convertible coming in at $4,222. Not even the higher prices dissuaded eager buyers, and 1960 saw more than 78,000 hardtops fly through the showrooms. Nearly 12,000 convertibles made their way into buyers' hands as well, making 1960 a record year for the Thunderbird.

1961–1963: The Bullet Bird

WITH THREE RECORD YEARS OF sales under its belt, Ford knew it was time to redesign its popular Thunderbird. The previous product cycle had allowed for only minor alterations to each subsequent year, and it was time for something new. George Walker, vice president of design at Ford, gave the final nod for a new Bird. With the space program at NASA well under way, the latest Thunderbird would echo the latest in space travel for the earthbound buyer. Boyer was once again given the task of conceiving the latest Thunderbird, and his talents were never more evident than with the newest design.

1961:
Out with the Square, In with the Bullet

THE SLEEK NEW design of the 1961 Thunderbird prompted enthusiasts to dub the model the Bullet Bird. Its introduction was wildly successful, and the era of the Square Bird came to a comfortable and timely close.

Although they were still being built using the proven unit-construction method of earlier models, the 1961 Thunderbird did not share a single inch of sheet metal with the previous year's. From stem to stern, the chassis was draped in a

ABOVE AND OPPOSITE: The aerodynamic styling of the 1961 T-Birds was perfectly suited to the blossoming space age—the long, rounded shape earned the cars the nickname "Bullet Birds." At the front end, the grille and bumper were combined.

FOLLOWING PAGES:
Power brakes, power steering, and automatic transmission became standard on the '61 Bird, catering to the tastes of luxury buyers. New round taillights sat below small fins on the 1961 Bird.

swoopy, tightly penned configuration. Several styling clues were carried over from the previous years, but even these familiar traits were given a fresher look. The hood of the 1961 was hinged at the rear, a first for the T-Bird.

The sculpted body panels added both style and substance to the latest iteration, and they were available in any of nineteen colors of the new, mildly metallic Diamond Lustre paint. Cars could be ordered in single colors or in one of thirty different two-tone variations, including seven reverse schemes.

Inside the fresh Bird, interior space was largely unchanged. A new option for 1961 was the Swing-Away steering wheel, which moved to allow for easier access into the trim-fitting cockpit. Upholstery options were

expanded and included several variations that incorporated vinyl, cloth, and even leather. Sixteen different combinations of six colors were listed. For the first time, the inside-mounted rearview mirror was glued directly to the windshield.

The 1961 models made a number of the previous years' options standard, and the new price reflected this by being $400 higher. A fully automatic top was also incorporated into the new standard design, making top-down motoring easier than ever.

With all the new improvements, the Thunderbird was also given a larger engine. The 352-cubic-inch motor was enlarged to 390. Although horsepower remained at 300, the torque was bumped to 427 foot-pounds from 381, giving the car a feeling of superior power. The engine was fitted with a new automatic choke and exhaled through a dual

exhaust system. Underneath, additional rubber bushings were implemented to improve both ride and handling.

The dramatic new Thunderbird was chosen to be the official pace car at the Indianapolis 500 that year, a crowning achievement for the sleek two-door.

1962:
The T-Bird Flock Grows by Two

STYLING ON THE 1962 Thunderbird was mostly unchanged, but two new models were added to the lineup. Both the Sports Roadster and the Landau presented the potential buyer with variations on a T-Bird theme, offering the same basic body with two very distinctive roof styles.

A few revisions that applied to the entire Thunderbird lineup were of the cosmetic nature. The all-horizontal front grille trim had been altered to include a series of chrome buttons, and the taillights were also fitted with new chrome trim. The previous stack of four chrome blades on the rear quarter panels was replaced with three horizontal bars.

The new Landau was simply a dressier version of the existing hardtop, decked out with attractive features that lent an additional air of luxury to the already classic lines of the Thunderbird. The roof of the Landau was covered in textured fabric, which was available in black or white, and adorned with S-shaped landau bars. These chromed trim pieces really set the Landau apart from the other models on the showroom floor.

Inside, the Landau was also fitted with trim pieces that were found exclusively in this model. Although it was not a runaway best-seller, sales for the Landau helped boost sales for T-Bird hardtops by almost 5,000 units in 1962.

But the real showstopper in the 1962 catalog was the new Sports Roadster. Ever since the demise of the original two-seater Thunderbird, many buyers longed for the return of the more intimate configuration. Budget

restraints being what they were, there was no way that Ford could build a two-seater version of the Thunderbird for such a small number of buyers. In response to the demands of the market, the Sports Roadster was created to fill the void.

After the convertible roof of this four-seater was lowered, the sleek tonneau cover was attached, and voilà, a two-seater was born. The rear seats remained in place but were covered by the fiberglass housing, which fit snugly around each of the front bucket seats, giving the illusion of a real sports car without sacrificing the utility of the rear seats. And by folding the front passenger seat forward, small items could be

ABOVE: The cockpit of the 1962 T-Birds enhanced the fighter-plane feel as it flowed around both the driver and passenger. It was a hit with customers seeking an earthbound jet plane.

stored in the rear section, creating a bit of additional cargo space even when the top was hiding the back seat.

In addition to the tonneau cover, the rear wheel skirts were removed on the Sports Roadster. Although the opened wheel wells were somewhat less graceful than on the other T-Birds, they allowed the roadster's unique wire wheels to be used without obstruction.

The Thunderbird Sports Roadster was well received, but the $5,500 price tag limited the sales to fewer than 1,500 for the year.

Another choice available to the buyer of any 1962 Thunderbird was the M-code power plant. While still displacing the same 390 cubic inches of the standard engine, the M was fitted with a trio of two-barrel carburetors. This combination produced an extra 40 horsepower and looked as impres-

sive at it ran. Despite the additional power the M-code delivered, only a few hundred were sold that year, making it a rare vehicle.

Along with the other improvements, larger brakes were hung at each corner of the Thunderbird, which helped to slow down the heavier model from cruising speeds with an extra measure of confidence.

Two-tone color combinations numbered twenty-one for the year, as Detroit seemed determined to be able to build a different car for every buyer. Interior options included vinyl, Bedford cloth, and leather, and Diamond Blue entered the color charts later in the model year, making nineteen different combinations of color and fabric available to the Thunderbird buyer.

By adding the two new models to the lineup and revising the entire collection, Ford saw record numbers for the T-Bird in 1962. Sales reached nearly 80,000 for the year, with the hardtop and Landau models claiming almost 90 percent of the total.

BELOW: Pictured here is the '62 Sports Roadster, seen from the rear. FOLLOWING PAGES: Fitted with the hard tonneau cover, the Sports Roadster model offered the look and feel of a two-seater in a four-seater configuration.

1963:
The Birds Struggle Against Competitors

FOR MANY YEARS, THE THUNDERBIRD filled the niche for a functional yet sporty vehicle. Attempts by competitors to break into Thunderbird territory never seemed to cut into sales. But by 1964 the scene was changing. The Grand Prix and Riviera from General Motors were beginning to erode the sales of the venerable Thunderbird, and Ford was forced to make changes in an attempt to slow the decline.

The graceful side panels of the 1962 were augmented with a sweeping body line sculpted into the steel for the '63 model. A set of three parallelogram-shaped trim pieces was positioned on each door, replacing the trio of horizontal bars on the rear quarter panels. The front grille area was filled with a row of fine vertical bars, aiding the flowing lines of the entire design.

Efforts were made to quiet the somewhat noisy Thunderbird by increasing the amount of sound-deadening materials used in construction. The more luxurious Thunderbird kept the driver and passengers coddled in a more peaceful environment. The quieter cabin allowed the occupants to enjoy the newest option, an AM/FM radio. Exterior finishes were still numerous, and there were plenty of interior choices.

The instrument panel could be complemented by the optional tachometer for 1963. Engine choices remained the same, but an alternator took the place of the previous generator under the hood. Despite relatively few changes, the price for the standard Bird increased by about $125.

Meanwhile, the Landau was growing in popularity, and the interior was treated to simulated wood trim, including the mock wooden steering wheel. In addition to the standard Landau, a special edition was introduced during the 1963 model year, trimmed in Corinthian White paint and topped off with a Rose Beige vinyl top. The extra-heavy texture of the roof material enhanced the chrome landau bars on each sail panel. The interior was finished in white leather, with accents of Rose Beige to match the roof. Only 2,000 examples of this model were offered, and they sold for the handsome fee of $4,748 each. The car's elegant design and feminine color palate—along with the fact that its premiere was held in Monaco—led to the car's nickname, The Princess Grace.

Despite all of Ford's efforts, Thunderbird sales were slipping badly. Just over 63,000 copies of the Bird were sold in 1963, a far cry from the nearly 80,000 sold the year before. The Sports Roadster suffered the largest loss—total sales never reached 500. Only 37 of those sold were fitted with the potent M-code engines.

The final year of the product cycle for the Bullet Birds was 1963, and Ford harbored great hopes of regaining its dominance in this segment of the market with the next generation of Thunderbirds.

ABOVE AND OPPOSITE:
The Thunderbirds of 1963 can be easily identified by the sharp crease in the flowing bodywork, accented by the trio of parallelograms of chrome below it, as on the convertible (above) and the Sports Roadster (opposite).

RIGHT: A console-mounted tachometer allowed the driver to closely monitor the action underneath the hood. OPPOSITE: A bank of three two-barreled carburetors helped to boost the M-code engine to a rating of 340 horsepower.

....

ABOVE: The crisp yet graceful lines of the hardtop do nothing to detract from the overall design of the 1963 models. OPPOSITE: The year 1964 saw the introduction of the next generation of Thunderbird, and its crisp bodywork was the natural extension of the previous examples. The jet-exhaust taillights were replaced with large rectangular units for the next line of Thunderbirds, and they did a fine job of capping off the sharper lines of the '64s.

1964–1966: A Fourth Generation of Birds

WITH A YEAR OF FALLING sales still fresh on their minds, Ford brass had pinned great hopes on the fourth generation of Thunderbirds. The competition was still drawing away customers, so the new Bird had to be more than some fresh sheet metal.

1964:
In with the New—and a Bit of the Old

WITH THE FIRST APPEARANCE OF the 1964 model, it was obvious that the Ford design team had done their homework. The new car represented a marriage of new features and family heritage, and despite the many improvements, it remained instantly recognizable as a Thunderbird. From the swept-back "eyebrows" above the headlights to the all-new rectangular taillights, there was fresh blood flowing through the T-Bird's veins. The more angular bodywork echoed that of the popular Square Bird and proved to be a strong selling point.

The symmetrical lines of the bodywork culminated in a nearly flat trunk surface devoid of the earlier fins. The

deeply sculpted side panels flowed smoothly and gave the '64 a look of muscular elegance. The air scoop of the car's hood, which had become a Thunderbird trademark, was made even larger. The fresh design also allowed for bigger doors for more comfortable entry into and exit from the sumptuous interior.

Once inside the '64, the driver was greeted by the flight-deck instrument panel that housed the gauges in individual pods, all of which glowed green at night. This tack proved to be a huge selling point for the latest version, as drivers pictured themselves flying their new T-Birds over the interstates. Safety features were abundant, and even the two-spoke steering wheel wore a padded hub to protect the driver in the event of an accident. The Silent-Flo ventilation system allowed fresh air to enter the cockpit at the front window, move silently through the car, and exit at the base of the rear window. The side vent windows could also be cranked open manually to assist in the movement of air.

With only three models remaining on the T-Bird roster for 1964, the Sports Roadster became a thing of the past. The convertible Bird could still be fitted with a hard tonneau cover for $269, but the feature didn't work as well as it had on the Sports Roadsters. The latest convertible top was even easier to use, though when stowed away it took up most of the trunk space. The hardtop and Landau models completed the triangle of available Birds and made up most of the recorded sales. They were available in a choice of twenty different single colors at the outset of the model year, with Prairie Bronze and Sunlight Yellow joining the list later.

Power for the Thunderbird was supplied by a single engine for 1964. The 390-cubic-inch, 300-horsepower V8 proved to be an adequate source of energy, despite the weight gain of 300 pounds (136kg) for the '64. A bigger, 20-gallon (76L) fuel tank meant longer distances between fill-ups.

The fourth generation of Thunderbirds proved to be a phenomenal success. Sales of the 1964 Thunderbird outstripped the previous year's model by nearly 30,000 and came close to eclipsing the standing record set in the 1960 model year, when more than ninety thousand Birds were sold. After a year of having its wings clipped, the Thunderbird was back in flight.

1965:
The Sophomore Jinx

AFTER A BLOCKBUSTER YEAR OF sales in 1964, Ford decided to make only minor modifications to its again-popular Thunderbird. Even the price remained the same, a tactic aimed at keeping the customers flocking to the showrooms. But in what would become a pattern for the Bird, sales began to slump in the second year of the iteration.

The bodywork for the '65 was unchanged, but chrome brightwork was added, moved, and replaced. The front grille insert was comprised of a mesh surface divided by six intersecting vertical bars. Similar vertical dividers were found on the existing taillight lenses, carrying the design trend through. The most noticeable addition was the simulated vents on each front quarter panel. Ford coined them "wastegates," but they were nothing more than trim.

Another new feature on the '65 was the sequential turn signals at the tail end. When either signal was activated, a series of three lights flashed from inside to outside, notifying other drivers of your intentions and really

impressing your neighbors. This feature would eventually show up on other Ford products, but this was the first-ever application.

ABOVE: Nineteen sixty-five would be another year of subtle improvements for the Thunderbird, as seen in this pristine Landau. RIGHT: The sharper lines of the 1965 interior echoed the tighter creases in the external bodywork.

The list of available options continued to change like the weather as Ford tried to offer the most tempting features for the discriminating buyer. The old standby, blackwall tires, could be ordered with either white or red stripes for an additional $44. Disc brakes were available on the front axle of the Thunderbird, which really enhanced stopping capabilities. (The addition of the disc brakes eliminated the wire wheels from the options list because they were not compatible with the new brake design.)

Those opting for the convertible model found the hard tonneau cover was no longer offered. However, many dealers found themselves with leftover inventory from the previous year, which helped to fulfill some of the remaining demand.

The Landau was still in the nest, and a special edition was also listed. The Limited Edition Special Landau was finished in a coat of Ember-Glo paint and paired with a

contrasting Parchment vinyl roof. The wheel covers were trimmed with accents of Ember-Glo, as was the interior. A special plaque inside this Landau was emblazoned with the owner's name. This entire package sold for only $50 more than the standard Landau, which played heavily into the fact that 4,500 were sold.

Other examples of the Thunderbird could be painted in one of twenty-six colors, with a selection of thirty-five choices of interior trim. As always, the Thunderbird was not a car for the indecisive buyer.

Yet despite the many improvements and the previous year's formidable sales, sales of the 1965 Thunderbird fell by nearly 18,000 units for the model year, with only about 75,000 rolling out the showroom doors. It was obvious that America's attention span was growing shorter, and hopes were once again pinned on the upcoming generation of Birds to rekindle the flame.

1966:
One Last Gasp

WITH 1966 BEING THE LAST of the three-year product cycle, changes to the Thunderbird were kept to a minimum. Of course, Ford hoped for another great year of sales, but after losing eighteen thousand customers in 1965, the company was not about to hold its breath.

Once again, the basic bodywork remained unchanged. The grille was given a mild reshaping and filled with a rectangular grating. The pseudo air vents were once again gone from the front fenders, leaving nothing behind. Rear wheel skirts were no longer standard equipment, but each of the wheel wells was trimmed with a fine chrome strip. On a Thunderbird ordered with the skirts, the rear wells were devoid of the chrome trim. At the back end, the taillight panel stretched completely across the car, with the backup lights sandwiched between the pair of rectangular signals. Sequential turn indicators remained a key feature.

In the horsepower department, an optional engine was finally offered. The standard 390-cubic-inch motor produced 315 horsepower, and the next step was the latest 428-cubic-inch option. This larger choice delivered 345 horsepower as well as additional torque. It cost less than $100 to add this selection, and many buyers opted to do so.

The interior was once again available with a new variety of options. Cruise control appeared as Highway Pilot Control, and the device made long days in the saddle a little more comfortable. While you were traveling down the road, you also had the luxury of listening to your favorite 8-track tapes on the AM radio/8-track unit, available for the first time. For the ultimate in luxury, the interior could be draped in leather for an additional $147. This option also included a reclining passenger seat.

Two fresh faces were added to the team for 1966. The Town Hard Top and Town Landau models featured a sail panel that was stretched to meet the trailing edge of the front door. Although the panel added an additional measure of elegance to the appearance, it reduced the driver's rear view. The Town versions of the T-Bird were also mated with an overhead warning light console, an option on the standard hardtops.

BELOW: Ford compared the 1966 Thunderbird to an airplane, but the new Bird didn't quite fly off of showroom floors.

The Thunderbird Touch:
An overhead Safety Convenience Panel

1966 Thunderbird Town Landau with new formal roofline

Look! Thunderbird for 1966 has a unique Safety-Convenience Panel, mounted overhead on Town Hardtop and Landau models. Tap a switch and the Emergency Flasher System sets four exterior lights blinking. Other lights remind you to fasten seat belts, tell you when fuel is low, or doors ajar. Other personal Thunderbird touches for 1966 include the optional AM Radio/Stereo-sonic Tape system to give you over 70 minutes of music on an easy-to-load tape cartridge. Completely automatic! Four speakers! New, too, are: an automatic Highway Pilot speed control option; more powerful standard V-8—plus a 428 cubic inch optional V-8. And all the craftsmanship that has made this car a classic in its own time.

Thunderbird
UNIQUE IN ALL THE WORLD

As limited as the Town Landau made the driver's ability to see, this new iteration accounted for about half of all Thunderbirds sold that year. The consumer was voting for luxury over practicality, and the tally was proof enough.

Just as the Town versions bowed, the convertible was about to make its final appearance. Sales of the convertible Bird reached only 5,049 for the year, as people became accustomed to riding in climate-controlled comfort, safe from the elements.

In Ford's gallant attempt to stem lost sales, the price of the Thunderbirds actually dropped for 1966. Despite these efforts, sales continued to slip, and only about 69,000 Birds were delivered.

ABOVE: With the cloth top stowed away, the 1966 Birds had one of the cleanest profiles in the business. RIGHT: Accented by an enormous Thunderbird emblem, the front grille was also found in a much more angular position.

CHAPTER TWO

FROM SPORTS TO LUXURY

DURING THE LATE SIXTIES and early seventies, the Thunderbird underwent a subtle but undeniable transformation, as sports car styling and performance were sacrificed for more glamorous and luxurious appointments.

1967–1969: The Fifth Generation

HAVING HAD ONLY ONE GOOD year out of the previous three, by 1967 the Thunderbird was due for a serious makeover. The car-buying public's reaction to luxury and style over sportiness and fun was not lost on Ford. While earlier designs had carefully straddled the old and the new, the '67 models were drawn on a clean sheet of paper.

1967:
The Newest Bird
Takes Flight

THE NAIL IN the coffin of the Thunderbird as a sports car came with the elimination of the convertible from the T-Bird lineup. To replace the drop-

PAGES 46–47: A 1976 Landau. RIGHT: The control panel of the 1966 T-Bird looked downright boxy when compared to other models. OPPOSITE: The cockpit-like interior and center console became trademarks of the late-sixties Thunderbird. PAGES 50–51: The Landau coupe was the two-door iteration of the big 1967 T-Bird.

Four-Door "Suicide"

Legend has it that when Lee Iacocca saw the first sketches for a four-door Bird, he became so enamored of the idea that he ordered Ford's stylists to complete the design as quickly as they could. Central to the design, which debuted in the 1967 model year, was the use of what were widely known as "suicide doors": the second set of doors was hinged at the back end, so that the front and back door handles were placed side by side. The design was a throwback to the 1930s, but those earlier attempts had proven quite dangerous, due to the poor latching mechanisms available at the time. With a propensity to opening while the car was in motion, anyone unlucky enough to be holding on to the door panel was usually thrown from the vehicle, inspiring the "suicide" moniker that stuck with the design long after the danger had been eliminated. But the new design was far from suicidal for Ford—the new four-door sold briskly, with almost 25,000 four-door Birds flying off the showroom floors that first year.

top model, a larger, four-door sedan was added. The design for the four-door was a culmination of efforts between two separate design teams and was given the final go-ahead from Ford chief Lee Iacocca himself.

The entire Thunderbird trio rode on a body-on-frame layout in an effort to trim construction costs. The two- and four-door cars each had a different wheelbase but shared a common central chassis. The ends of the structure were determined by the model ordered. The all-new body was suspended on fourteen individual mounts to isolate the driver and passengers from noise, vibration, and a harsh ride. The wheels themselves were cushioned by coil springs at all four corners, which gave the Thunderbird its most compliant ride ever.

S P E C S

1967 Thunderbird

Weight
4,256 lbs.
(1932.2kg)

Engine type
V8, 90 degree,
OHV

Engine displacement
390 ci

Horsepower
315

Transmission
three-speed automatic

Wheelbase
115 in. (229.1cm)

Overall length
206.9 in.(523.2cm)

Overall width
77.3 in. (196.3cm)

Overall height
54.6 in.(138.7cm)

Exterior colors
twenty single colors,
thirty-five two-tone
combinations

Interior colors
seven

Options
428 ci engine, vinyl top,
four-door Landau,
warning light cluster,
leather interior

Total production
24,967

The four-door Landau wheelbase measured just over 117 inches (297cm), while the two-door models came in at just under 115 inches (292cm). The rear doors of the sedan opened toward the back of the car, a styling feature known as the "suicide" design. With little support between them, the doors were at first thought to be quite dangerous in the event of a collision, but they turned out to be no more than a styling effort, and no actual deaths were ever attributed to their use.

The interior of the 1967 was also brand-new. The seats, console, door panels, and dash were all restyled for this fifth generation of Thunderbirds. While retaining some of the earlier space-age feel, the instrument panel was toned down a bit and slid toward the side of luxury. The Swing-Away, the steering wheel that could be shifted only laterally, was replaced by the Tilt-Away, which moved in two directions to allow for easier entry.

Styling on the outside was a radical departure from any previous Thunderbird, with the exception of the sail pan-

els, which bore a vague resemblance to those on earlier models. The oval front end treatment included hideaway headlights for the first time.

At the aft end of the longer, wider Bird, there were taillights that once again spanned the entire width of the car and flashed sequentially. The Diamond Lustre paints were upgraded to Super Diamond Lustre for 1967, and twenty different choices were available. A wide selection of interior trim was also listed, allowing a buyer to tailor his Thunderbird to exacting standards. Power train changes were nil for the new model, and the buyer could still choose between the 390- and 428-cubic-inch motors. The three models sold well, with the two-door Landau taking first place with more than 37,000 registered sales. The all-new four-door Landau sedan came in second with a respectable 25,000 units,

ABOVE: After the successful introduction of the four-door Bird, Ford didn't want to jinx themselves with a sweeping revision. The 1968 was little different from its older siblings.

Double
Thunder

Top. 1968 Thunderbird 2-door Hardtop.   Bottom. 1968 Thunderbird 4-door Landau.
This year, double excitement: You can fly the roomy new 4-door Bird
or a racy 2-door Bird. Both with the scorching new 429-cu. in. V-8
to thunder you across the landscape. Choose optional buckets or new standard
full-width front seats. Room for 4, 5, or 6. Option after option after option.
Get double your share of action this year. Fly the Bird.

'68 Thunderbird
unique in all the world.

ABOVE: Advertisements for the late-60s Birds were directed at middle-class drivers seeking luxury. Ads for the '68 highlighted the choice of two configurations for the latest Bird and the long list of options that made the cars among the most customizable around.

and the plain-Jane hardtop racked up nearly 16,000 units sold. All told, 1967 turned out to be the fourth-best year in history for Thunderbird sales.

1968:
Subtle Changes for the New Model

IN 1968, FOR the first time in its history, Thunderbird production was completed in two different facilities: the Michigan factory was joined by a sister plant in California. After recording another decent year of sales, the '68 Bird was gifted with only minor enhancements. Most of the changes were of Ford's origination, but a few were results of new government legislation that mandated certain safety features.

The first of many federally required changes was the addition of the side marker lights. Small rectangular lenses were illuminated on the front quarter panels, while the rear-mounted markers were simply reflectors. In the interest of safety, shoulder harnesses became standard equipment. To increase safety in the event of a frontal impact, many components of the interior were more heavily padded to absorb the energy created during an accident.

In addition to federally mandated changes, Ford implemented a number of smaller changes in 1968. The large front grille went unchanged in shape and size but was filled with larger rectangular openings. The single Thunderbird logo of 1967 was replaced by a pair of smaller Birds, one on each headlight cover. The front bumper was made narrower and consisted of two pieces, one of which housed the parking lights.

Three basic models remained, and a Town Sedan appeared later in the year. Featuring a painted roof in place of the vinyl padded variety, it still came adorned with the swooping-S trim pieces. Changes in the layout of the interior for all the Birds allowed for seating of five adults versus only four. Bucket seats—with a center console—could still be had if desired, but the new benches allowed for three people in both the front and the rear.

Alongside the existing 390-cubic-inch motor came a much larger 429 Thunderjet option. Packing 360 horses, it soon became the only selection, as the 390 was eliminated in January 1968.

Of the twenty colors available in 1968, ten were carryovers, but variations of colors, interior choices, and options remained plentiful.

The latest round of changes failed to increase sales, and 13,000 fewer units were actually sold for the 1968 model year. With a total of fewer than 65,000 cars sold, the figures were the lowest since 1963. This was not the trend that Ford management had hoped for.

1969:
Final Year, Minor Changes

THE YEAR 1969 WAS ONCE again the last of the three years in the typical product cycle, and big changes were in the works for the 1970 models. Engineering resources were deferred

toward the all-new Bird, soon to be seen. Proving itself to be an on-again, off-again sales performer, the Thunderbird underwent only minor modifications for 1969.

In typical fashion, the front end was given a fresh grille arrangement. The new grille was die-cast versus the usual assortment of smaller pieces fitted together. A heavy horizontal bar was intersected by three thinner vertical bars, and each of the resulting rectangles was filled with a ribbed background. Given the same texture as the grille, the headlight doors were virtually invisible within the network.

The taillights, which had spanned the entire rear end for years, became two separate rectangular lenses. The signals still featured sequential flashing. The panel bridging the two lenses was solid, with no illumination at all. The side

marker lights and reflectors were altered to be slightly smaller but still conformed to the latest government regulations for improved visibility.

The 429-cubic-inch engine remained as the only source of motivation but continued to provide ample horsepower for the big Bird. Breathing through dual exhausts, the latest variation of the big 429 required the use of premium fuel only.

Confronting the wails of drivers almost everywhere, the 1969 Thunderbird rode on suspension that provided far better handling and control. Although much stiffer than previous years, the compliant, comfort-

ABOVE: In 1969, the "new" Thunderbirds were once again simply modified versions of previous models, a fact that was beginning to send buyers into the competitor's showrooms.

able ride was still present, and an added degree of control was evident.

A return of the sunroof—now operated electrically rather than manually—offered the owner fresh-air motoring at the touch of a switch. The large opening let plenty of sunshine in without a lot of fuss or buffeting. Last available on the 1960 models, the 1969 application seemed to be of a far better design, and the new option cost an additional $453.

Ford's earlier domination of this segment of the market was rapidly slipping, and with every passing year Thunderbird was losing more and more sales to competing cars—and the competition was growing. In previous years, the Bird's only real competition came from General Motors' camp in the form of the Monte Carlo and the Riviera. But for 1969, Chrysler's Charger also slipped ahead of the T-Bird in sales. The Charger, sold by Dodge, outsold the Bird largely on the basis of price, making it obvious that Ford needed to infuse the next Bird with a real dose of excitement as well as a level of affordability in order to reassert itself as the premier car manufacturer in the United States.

Just over 49,000 units were produced for the 1969 model year, the lowest figure since 1958. The next Thunderbird proved that Ford was not ready to give up on its once-successful model.

1970–1971: The Bunkie Beak T-Bird

THE SIXTH GENERATION of Thunderbirds was interesting, if somewhat short-lived—it survived for only two years.

1970:
The Knudsen Effect

DUE TO THE RESULTS OF unusual timing, the first Thunderbird to carry any influence from legendary auto executive Semon E. "Bunkie" Knudsen appeared after he had left the Ford nest. It was his input that caused the sixth generation of Birds to grow a distinct protrusion, or Bunkie Beak, as the press had dubbed it.

While riding on a chassis that was largely unchanged from the previous generation, the Thunderbird was dressed in fresh sheet metal and hosted many new features. The body/chassis isolation was still a highly effective method of separating the occupants from road defects, and an additional quantity of sound-deadening material made the cockpit even quieter.

Up front, the obvious change was the enormous nose that sprouted from the long lines of the hood. This was Knudsen's attempt to make the Thunderbird look more like its General Motors counterpart. GM's Grand Prix had been fitted with a similar proboscis and was turning out to be one of the Thunderbird's biggest competitors. The two sets of dual headlights were exposed, no longer involved in the peekaboo setup. The bank of sequential taillight lamps once again traversed the entire width of the tail and was executed in a sleek new format.

The overall length of the 1970 model had grown by 6 inches (15cm) and also rode 1 inch (2.5cm) lower to the ground. This new stature gave the Thunderbird an exaggerated look of being even longer than it really was.

There were many minor changes to the '70 that gave it a cleaner profile, including the in-glass radio antenna and hidden windshield wipers. Inside, the standard front seat had become a bench, with bucket seats and a console being a $78 option. The Tilt-Away wheel was removed from the hardware list and replaced with a simpler tilt wheel.

Total production remained flat, barely exceeding 50,000 units. Of these, almost 37,000 were of the Landau coupe variety. Despite the dwindling production numbers, the Thunderbird actually saw an increase in its share of the market over the 1969 figures.

1971:
One Down, One to Go

THE BUNKIE BEAK DESIGN WAS never well received, and Ford was obviously resistant to throw good money after bad. The 1971 Thunderbirds were little more than 1970s with very minor trim changes.

Among the changes were the revised trim on the grille, slightly larger bumper ends, and a few available options. One reasonably exciting option package was the Turnpike

An Expensive Nose Job

The addition of the "Bunkie Beak" was more than an aesthetic shock. Protruding out precariously ahead of the rest of the car, the distinctive nose of the 1970–71 Bird seemed like an accident waiting to happen. As a result, auto insurers felt justified in increasing collision premiums on the cars, claiming that the awkward nose was extremely vulnerable to damage in the event of a collision. In fact, accident records show that the nose wasn't particularly fragile or accident-prone, although the costly parts meant that accident claims were fairly high. In the end, it wasn't a compromised front end that did in the Bunkie Beak, but declining sales and a changing market.

Convenience Group. This bundle of options included cruise control, a reclining front seat, and steel-belted radial tires.

Two models remained in the Thunderbird nest for 1971, but declining sales made this the last year for the Landau sedan. The number of units had been dropping each year, and Ford finally decided to pull the plug on the big four-door. Of the two remaining models, the Landau coupe was outselling its hardtop brethren by more than two to one despite its higher cost. Both versions of the hardtop body featured a wider sail panel that looked great but hampered side vision. It was obvious that people preferred style over substance, as sales grew for these two cars regardless of their shortcomings in the visibility department.

Ford knew it needed to resurrect the sales of the once-great Thunderbird and called upon the styling direction and input of Lee Iacocca for the rescue process. The year 1972 would see the first signs of his efforts, which would push the Thunderbird back into record territory in only a few short years.

1972–1976: The Big Birds

THE ORIGINAL THUNDERBIRD HAD BEEN targeted at the sports car driver and was appointed in attire fitting for the task. As the years progressed, the Thunderbird was weaned from its sports car roots, becoming more and more of a cruising car. By 1972, the metamorphosis was complete; the new model was a luxury vehicle for the masses, without the slightest hint of the Bird's sporty past.

1972:
The New Luxury Birds

WITH LEE IACOCCA AT THE helm of Ford, the decision was made to take the Thunderbird on a new tack, and any resemblance to the sporty Bird of yesteryear was gone. Even the four-door Landau was banished, leaving only one model in the Thunderbird lineup. This model mirrored its larger cousin, the Lincoln Mark IV, sharing many of the same components.

The 1972 Thunderbird rode on a wheelbase of 120.4 inches (306cm), almost 6 inches (15cm) longer than the previous year's model. Length had blossomed to an overall measurement of 216 inches (549cm), just 4 inches (10cm) shy of the Mark IV. A bare-bones Bird tipped the scales at 4,503 pounds (2,044kg) but few, if any, cars were delivered in this trim. The base price of the latest models had also grown to nearly $5,300. But the majority of '72 Birds were delivered at costs much closer to $7,000—the plethora of available options proved too tempting for most buyers, who loaded up their Birds before taking flight.

The latest body rode on an all-new perimeter chassis and was complemented by an upgraded suspension. High praise was given by most of the motoring press on the level of comfort delivered by the new setup. Another advancement was the availability of the Sure Track braking system. In actuality, it was an early attempt at antilock brakes, and it helped to maintain control of the rear binders during panic stops.

Engine options consisted of the standard 429 V8, rated at 212 net horsepower, and the larger 460-cubic-inch variant, which delivered 224 net horsepower. The new ratings for horsepower were a bit of an aberration because the cars were still quite fast for their bulk. Fuel consumption suffered with the new heft, and many owners would register little more than an average of 10 miles per gallon (1.6km per 3.7L) in their new Thunderbirds.

The latest generation was well received and sales figures reflected the confidence of buyers. Almost 58,000 examples of the 1972 Thunderbird were sold in the first year of the five-year production cycle.

Ford also built its one millionth Thunderbird during the 1972 model year and assembled a single commemorative Bird to celebrate the event. Trimmed in gold and labeled accordingly, that car remains one of the most coveted T-Birds ever produced.

1973:
Luxury Refined

AN ALL-NEW Thunderbird had appeared to the world in 1972, and

OPPOSITE: Due to the mostly unloved "beak" on the 1970 and 1971 models, the 1972s would appear with a wider version of the pointy grille.

57

a year later Ford once again followed up with only minor refinements.

The front end was fitted with a larger bumper, due to federal mandates on safety during 5-mile-per-hour (8kph) crashes. The grille was comprised of a rectangular grate system in lieu of the previous horizontal bar design. The headlights were once again housed in their own individual rectangles, giving the nose a distinct five-box look. A stand-up hood ornament helped to give the latest Bird a look of stately elegance.

Additional protection was provided by the wider body-side moldings, which were keyed to the chosen color. Early in the model year, opera windows were offered as an option. These openings allowed for greater visibility through the Landau roof and became standard in June. The taillights remained in their ever-popular full-width mode and provided even more visibility to those traveling behind you.

The 1973 catalog showed fifteen standard color choices along with eight Glamour colors—paints that contained a higher level of metallic particles and really sparkled in the bright sunshine. Steel-belted radial whitewall tires finally became a standard item. Although the changes seemed minor, the price on the T-Bird had risen dramatically, with a base sticker price of more than $6,400. Yet sales marched into new territory: nearly 30,000 more Thunderbirds were sold in 1973 than in 1972. It was obvious that the American consumer was adjusting well to the new variation on the Thunderbird theme.

1974:
The Fuel Crisis Curtails Sales

THE 1974 THUNDERBIRD WAS BARELY altered from the previous year, but—with the nation in the midst of an unprecedented fuel shortage—sales fell dramatically. As drivers waited in unfathomably long lines for rationed gasoline and wished they were filling the tanks of smaller, more fuel-efficient cars, they began to reevaluate their need for big, fuel-hungry cars like the overgrown Bird of 1974.

Still powered by the mammoth 460-cubic-inch V8, the fuel consumption of the Bird did nothing to help sales. Although managed by solid-state electronics, the Thunderbird had ballooned in size and weight. The overall length of the '74 had grown to 222 inches (564cm), and curb weight was up by more than 500 pounds (227kg). The fuel tank was enlarged to hold an additional 4 gallons (15L) of the precious cargo, which helped to carry the owner a bit farther between fill-ups, but that didn't help much in those fuel-hungry times: the average Thunderbird got only 11 miles per gallon (18km per 3.7L) of gasoline.

The 1973 Thunderbird.
In appearance,
in appointments, it's a luxury car.
In ride and handling,
it's distinctly Thunderbird.

The automobile that is known for ride and luxury has even more to offer this year.
Its suspension system has been refined and tuned to its steel-belted radial ply tires. Tires that are tested to give the average driver 40,000 miles of tread life in normal driving. Result: an extraordinarily smooth ride.
Some other special luxuries: cushioned front seats with twin center armrests. The comfortable efficiency of Thunderbird's power brakes and power steering. The classic look of its new optional Opera Window. Experience it at your Ford Dealer's.

A unique luxury automobile
THUNDERBIRD
FORD DIVISION *Ford*

The new 1973 Thunderbird pictured above also includes as standard equipment new energy-absorbing bumpers with bumper guards, left-hand remote control mirror and white sidewalls. Other equipment shown is optional.

LEFT AND OPPOSITE: In addition to a long list of luxury features, the 1973 Bird was fashioned with glass opera windows—reminiscent of the porthole openings on the 1956 hardtop. Advertising for the '73 touted the new model as a luxury car, but continued to emphasize its sporty legacy.

Most of the styling remained untouched for 1974. The taillight array was segmented but still crossed the entire width of the back end. A large backup light filled the space between the two red lenses. Another bit of added glass was the optional moonroof. Previous versions of this feature consisted of a steel panel that was retracted electrically, but the new variant was formed from glass, allowing light to enter even while closed.

One of the least popular items to join the cars of 1974 was the seatbelt starter interlock. The result of a new federal mandate, this feature required the driver to fasten his or her seatbelt before the car could be started. This safety feature was very poorly received by the buying public, many of whom felt it represented an invasion of privacy and personal space by the government.

Although little had changed from the last model, the base price rose once again, this time to just over $7,000. When teamed up with the poor mileage, the fuel crisis, and the pesky seatbelts, it was no surprise to see sales fall to just over 58,000 for the year.

1975:
Twentieth Anniversary

THE TWENTIETH YEAR OF PRODUCTION for the Thunderbird was 1975, but the fuel crisis gave Ford little reason to celebrate. The world shortage of gasoline was drastically affecting the United States, and shoppers for new cars sought vehicles that would squeeze the most miles out of each valuable drop.

It was common for only minor changes to appear on the T-Bird each new year, and such was the case in 1975. With plummeting sales, it was hard to justify huge expenditures for a new design, and for the first time, a T-Bird production cycle ran longer than the usual three years. There were, however, a few modifications to the '75 Bird.

Overall length had grown to an unprecedented 225.6 inches (573cm), but weight gain was less than 10 pounds (4.5kg). Every unit built that year was considered an anniversary model, but there was also a special commemorative edition—essentially the same car but with special trim—produced to highlight the occasion. Luxury Color Groups were the height of automotive fashion, and several different choices were available to entice those who wanted a bit more exclusivity. Each of these groups featured a set of custom colors that was paired with accenting interior trim. The Jade Luxury Group was new for 1975 and offered several different combinations of paint and fabrics. The all-Jade option saw the entire car draped in shades of jade green, while other choices used contrasts of white to offset the brilliant green color. The Luxury Color Group proved to be one of Ford's most successful marketing strategies for the Bird; future models would see more such options as consumers expressed a desire for more bang for their buck.

The most important upgrade for 1975 was the availability of four-wheel disc brakes. The heaviest Thunderbird ever built could be slowed with confidence. The Sure Track antiskid system was still mounted to the rear brakes, adding an extra measure of safety to the new design.

Once again, the Thunderbird suffered huge losses in sales. With sales down almost 16,000 from the previous year, fewer than 43,000 total units were assembled.

1976:
The End of an Era

DESIGN AND CONSTRUCTION changes were few for the 1976 Thunderbird, but a proliferation of colors and options would guarantee it a place in the record books.

With a base price of $7,790, the Bird was $3,000 less than the Lincoln Mark IV but more expensive than some European competitors. Such increasing prices were becoming common for the U.S. car industry, a trend that would continue as the years passed.

Personal comfort and selection were fast becoming the driving force behind most buyers' decisions, and Ford was not blind to

RIGHT: The lines between the Thunderbird and the Lincoln Mark IV were beginning to blur, as the Bird adopted much of the same shapes as the more expensive offering.
INSET: Not only was the 1975 Thunderbird luxurious, it was also a good value when compared to other cars with the same level of trim. This fact was not lost on the marketing team at Ford, who touted the value of the new T-Bird in advertisements.

The 1975 Thunderbird.
Could it be the best
luxury car buy in America?

Decide for yourself. Besides the very specialness of Thunderbird itself, and the superb feel of Thunderbird's ride, there's more to consider. All those lavish extras that come standard: Air conditioning. An AM/FM multiplex radio. Opera windows. Steel-belted whitewall radial ply tires. Deluxe bumper group and cornering lights. Choose the optional Moonroof, and you can have it in silver or gold color. Be sure to see the two new 20th Anniversary Thunderbird Editions for 1975. They're in Silver and Copper.

Shown: 1975 Thunderbird with optional Copper Luxury Group, and convenience group.

The closer you look, the better we look.

THUNDERBIRD
FORD DIVISION

the trend. Inside the more luxurious Thunderbird, the owner could opt for several new electronic gadgets. A Quadrasonic stereo was available with AM/FM and even an 8-track player, bringing the world of high fidelity to the car buyer for the first time. In the arena of comfort, the driver could purchase the optional power lumbar support for his seat.

Four different styles of wheel covers could be ordered, along with the usual bank of colors and interior designs. In addition to the standard paint and interior options, the selection of Luxury Color Groups continued to flourish. For the '76 model year, there were four available groups. Creme and Gold, Lipstick, and Bordeaux were the more available combinations. A special Bicentennial option—dressed up in red, white, and blue trim—was applied to only thirty-two cars. At nearly $10,00, the special editions weren't all that popular, despite the excitement surrounding America's two-hundredth-birthday bash.

The more popular Lipstick option teamed a brilliant red finish with interior accoutrements of equal intensity. Several variations on this theme were available, similar to the Jade Luxury Group of the previous year, and allowed the buyer to custom-order the Thunderbird to match his preferences.

Considered to be the most luxurious Thunderbird ever built, the average selling price of the '76 was evidence enough to prove the point. Many cars, thoroughly appointed, were leaving the dealers' floors at nearly $12,000.

Although fewer Americans were buying cars, those who were had grown accustomed to the luxury that the Thunderbird offered, and sales remained strong. The final year of such lavish attention was 1976, which will always be thought of as one of the Thunderbird's finest years. Sales of the '76s were up about 10,000 for the year, as some people rushed to capitalize on their last chance of owning one of the Big Birds, as they had been aptly named.

The year 1977 once again proved to be a watershed one for the Thunderbird. A whole new design and pricing strategy propelled the next Thunderbird to heights never before seen.

PAGE 62–63: Some exotic two-tone paint schemes were being offered in the 1970s, and Ford's lineup was not excluded from this activity, as this 1976 Thunderbird attests.
RIGHT: Far removed from the initial Thunderbird format, the 1976 Bird carried no pretense of being svelte or sporty.

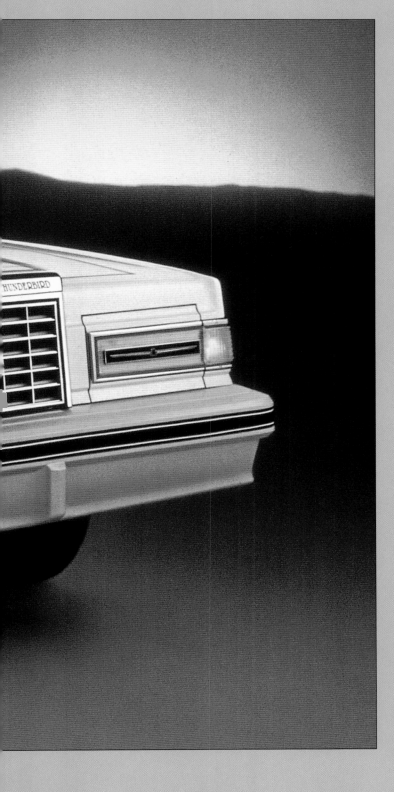

CHAPTER THREE

LEANER AND MEANER BIRDS

WITH LEE IACOCCA IN the captain's chair, changes were coming fast and furious at Ford. He wanted the Thunderbird to return to the days of being highly desired and began making the requisite changes to do just that.

Two of the criticisms of the last generation of Thunderbirds were the size of the car and the price. Over the years, the T-Bird had grown into an expensive, pseudo-luxury car that devoured fuel. Consumers may have loved the glamour of the Thunderbird, but not enough of them were coming forward with their checkbooks.

PAGES 66–67: For 1982, a new grille treatment was employed, along with several other minor enhancements. The only logo visible on the 1982 T-birds was the clear plastic hood ornament that was mounted atop the chrome surround of the grille. Chromed "Thunderbird" name badges were also included. OPPOSITE: The latter half of the 1970s saw nearly every auto manufacturer lose control of their ability to maintain any decorum in their designs. Sharp new lines on the Bird could be highlighted with fake trunk straps, as well as a host of other cosmetic blights.

1977–1979: Losing Weight and Gaining Sales

CHANGES TO THE CORPORATE AVERAGE FUEL Economy (CAFE) laws were enforced beginning in 1978, and the old, heavy Thunderbird was heavily penalized for its fuel-thirsty ways. This, along with changing consumer tastes, was enough impetus for Ford to enact a radical transformation for their Birds, making them lighter and more efficient.

1977: Record Sales for the New Bird

THE THUNDERBIRD THAT DEBUTED IN 1977 was nothing like the overweight fuel glutton that had preceded it. The new Bird was smaller and lighter, just what the fuel-conscious consumer of the late 1970s was looking for. It rolled on a wheelbase of only 114 inches (290cm), down more than 5 inches (13cm) from the 1976 model, and overall length was reduced by 10 inches (25cm); these and other changes resulted in an overall weight loss of 900 pounds (409kg). And if the savings at the pump weren't enough to entice consumers, the savings on the showroom floor were:

Lee Iacocca at Ford

His name is one of the most widely recognized in the American automotive industry, and for good reason. Lido Anthony "Lee" Iacocca started out selling Fords in Pennsylvania in the early 1950s, and by 1960 he was Ford's Division General Manager. He had an uncanny ability to read what the buying public wanted, and an even higher acuity at delivering it.

When in 1961 the company determined that the Ford lineup would benefit from the addition of a sporty two-seater, some suggested that the T-Bird should be reborn in its classic two-seat form of 1955–'57. But Iacocca insisted on an entirely different model. His instincts proved correct—the car that resulted was none other than the classic and still popular Mustang in 1964. Iacocca would later play the dominant role in shifting the Thunderbird into the "luxury" category and away from the "sporty" niche. The decision to build a four-door Thunderbird was based largely on Iacocca's insistence that there was a need for one. Huge sales for both the Mustang and the four door Bird were reason enough to boost Mr. Iacocca into the seat of the president's office by 1970.

Despite—or perhaps because of—his vision and his talent, Iacocca was quickly booted from the Ford ranks by none other than Henry Ford II. Known as a bit of a madman, "Henry the Deuce" didn't like being upstaged, and Iacocca had a knack for doing just that. But Iacocca wasn't one to go down easy. After his stint at Ford, he went on to turn the ailing Chrysler corporation around and became something of a corporate hero in the process.

RIGHT: To commemorate the arrival of another anniversary year, the Diamond Jubilee was rolled out for 1978. Decked out with a bevy of period accoutrements, the Jubilee was a rolling showcase of 1970s garish trim.

the sticker price of the 1977 Bird was down by nearly $3,000. The two-door hardtop listed for only $5,063, and the better-dressed Town Landau was only $7,990.

Sharing many design traits with Ford's LTD II, the Thunderbird was still grafted with many distinctive details that set it apart from its sister car. The most striking trim was the roof molding that encompassed the sail panels and top. The semirectangular opera windows were cut into this band and were highlighted with translucent Thunderbird logos. The headlights were hidden behind rotating panels, and the louvers gracing the front end were actually functional.

Underneath their lengthy hoods, the Thunderbirds were fitted with a new range of smaller, more efficient engines. The base model came equipped with the 302-cubic-inch V8. Emissions restrictions in California found cars bound for that state with cleaner-burning 351s mounted to their frames. In states other than California, buyers could get an optional 351 or 400. All three of these power plants were far more fuel-efficient than previous engines, yet they still delivered ample horsepower and torque. Not that drivers would be able to accurately measure the power—in response to yet another government regulation, the speedometer on the new models went up to only 85 miles per hour (137kph), despite the fact that the Thunderbird was capable of much higher speeds.

The combination of less weight, upgraded suspension, and a set of front and rear stabilizer bars made the 1977 Thunderbird one of the best-handling models ever. Braking was provided via front discs and rear drums.

All these improvements made an impact on sales. Over 318,000 units were sold. Production was handled by two plants—one in Wixom, Michigan, the second in Chicago, Illinois (the California factory was no longer utilized for T-Bird production). As both plants turned out thousands of cars to fill customer demands, it became apparent that after years of questionable performance, the Thunderbird was back on track.

S P E C S

1978 Thunderbird

Weight
4,082 lbs.
(1,853.2kg)

Engine type
V8, 90 degree, OHV

Engine displacement
302 ci

Horsepower
134

Transmission
Three-speed automatic

Wheelbase
114 in. (289.6cm)

Overall length
215.5 in. (547.4cm)

Overall width
78.5 in. (199.3cm)

Overall height
53 in. (134.6cm)

Exterior colors
Ten solids, twenty-one two-tone combinations

Options
351 ci engine, Sports Decor Group, T-top, Diamond Jubilee Edition, leather interior, front cornering lamps

Total production
352,751

1978:
The Rage Continues

THE RECENT VARIANT OF THE Thunderbird had proven itself to be one of the greatest sellers of all time for Ford. The seventy-fifth year of automotive production for Ford was 1978, and several special editions were built to commemorate the occasion.

Mechanical alterations on the 1978 Bird were minor, but that didn't stop people from flocking to the show-rooms in record numbers. The basic car was marked by the addition of a Thunderbird logo on each of the headlight covers. All other visible alterations came in the form of special-edition trim. The base price for the '78 models had increased almost $500 from the previous year, but that didn't stop Bird-hungry buyers.

To celebrate the seventy-fifth year of operations, Ford created the Diamond Jubilee Edition Thunderbird. Retailing for just over $10,000, it was chock-full of per-sonal touches. These cars were painted in colors that were specific to the Jubilees, and each door was monogrammed with the owner's initials. Inside the Diamond Jubilee, there was a twenty-two-carat gold plaque emblazoned with the owner's name. Other interior touches included velour upholstery, leather accents, and an AM/FM radio with power antenna. This list of special features was rather entic-ing, and nearly nineteen thousand people felt the increased cost was worth their money.

Another variation available was the Sports Decor Group. For about $400 more, the buyer was treated to a set of features found only on this model. The Sports Decor Group included a blacked-out front grille and a tan roof. The raised white-letter tires were mounted to cast spoke wheels, and the deck lid was adorned with a pair of mock luggage straps, complete with nonworking buckles.

Later in the model year, another option was made available for open-air motoring. Glass T-tops were fitted to the existing roofline and could be removed singly or in pairs to let the fresh air flow in. Once removed, the panels could be easily stowed in the trunk until the weather changed.

Even though the 1978 Thunderbird was mostly a carry-over from the previous year, it went on to set yet another record for sales: 352,751 copies found their way into consumers' garages, and it looked like Ford had given the Thunderbird a second lease on life.

1979:
T-Bird in Transition

THE BEGINNING OF THE NEW model year saw some drastic changes. The Thunderbird itself would remain largely the same, but the man credited with its rebirth would not fare as well. Just two years after he revived the seemingly hopeless Thunderbird, Lee Iacocca was relieved of his duties at Ford. He seemed to have a knack for lost causes, however—Iacocca went on to rescue Chrysler from the brink of collapse, and turned the failing company into a thriving firm.

Back on the T-Bird front, minor alterations were made as the sales continued to roll in at a steady pace. The grille of the '79 was adorned with a bolder design and encom-passed by a larger chrome surround. Additional touches of chrome were also implemented on the headlight covers, which sported even larger Thunderbird logos. The front quarter panels were adorned with a set of faux louvers just behind the wheel wells.

The previous full-width taillights had once again been converted into two separate lenses. Filling the void between the two signals was a large single-piece backup light. These were the only significant changes to the stan-dard Thunderbird, and most buyers opted for one of the special editions.

The luggage strap model, also known as the Sports Decor Group, was back for 1979. Different colors were offered, but the package remained the same. The Town Landau edition was positioned as the luxury-level T-Bird, and the lengthy list of standard features was evidence of its intentions.

A new variant for 1979 was the Heritage Edition. The most obvious change was the removal of the rear quarter window from the sail panels. In lieu of the glass, the thick-ly padded vinyl roof was highlighted with a script Heritage logo. The small opera window survived, providing a mini-mum of rearward vision for the driver.

The Heritage was available in either a maroon or a light medium blue color scheme. The chosen scheme would be

ABOVE: The bold new grille of the 1979 Thunderbird was flanked by rectangular covered headlights, each adorned with a large, chrome Thunderbird logo.

carried into the color-keyed wheels, grille, and bumper guards. Interior touches would help to accent the chosen theme. T-tops were once again offered as an option and carried a list price of $747. With no convertible model available, many chose this option to satisfy their need to feel the wind in their hair.

With sticker prices escalating rapidly, buyers were beginning to demand more value for their money and sought vehicles that would look new for a longer period. Extra measures of corrosion resistance were applied to all T-Birds, and buyers felt better about taking on the long-term loans required to cover the cost on a vehicle that they wouldn't want to replace too soon.

Standard power was again provided by the 302-cubic-inch motor, but it was fitted with an electronic voltage regulator and a more efficient two-barrel carburetor.

Thunderbirds were far from economy cars, but buyers knew this going into the deal. Although sales remained brisk, there was a precipitous drop in the figures. Compared to the more than 350,000 units sold the year before, the 284,000 units of 1979 seemed almost paltry. As it was the final year for this iteration, Ford once again hoped to draw the buyer back in to see and purchase the coming generation of Birds.

1980–1982: The Econobirds

SPEAKING IN GENERAL TERMS, THE early 1980s were difficult years for U.S. automakers. With the economy at a standstill, inflation raging out of control, and higher CAFE restrictions, consumers were taking a close look at where their hard-earned money should be spent.

1980:
Tarnished Silver Anniversary

IT MAY HAVE BEEN THE twenty-fifth anniversary of the Thunderbird, but there was little to celebrate. With sales declining, Ford needed a fresh new design and an economical package to draw buyers back to the T-Bird fold.

The 1980 T-Bird needed to be completely different from its predecessors, and with a team headed by legendary Ford designer Jack Telnack, it proved to be just that. With a stretched Fairmont chassis beneath it, the new Bird was 16 inches (41cm) shorter than the last version and more than 700 pounds (318kg) lighter. Even the ponderous width had been reduced by 4 inches (10cm) in an effort to produce a more efficient vehicle. Unit-body construction was once again implemented, the first use of this technology since 1966.

A leaner power plant was also installed to deliver more miles per gallon than the 1979s had. By reducing the bore of the standard 302 block, the new variant displaced only 255 cubic inches. A meager output of only 115 horsepower was the result of this effort, so the lighter weight of the Thunderbird was appreciated. An optional 302 was available, but even its horsepower rating hit only 131. A four-speed overdrive transmission was offered when purchasing the bigger 302, and the extra gear helped to deliver higher mileage with the more powerful engine.

To commemorate the twenty-fifth year of Thunderbird production, a silver anniversary model was created. Silver Glow paint was highlighted by touches of black, and the richly padded half-roof was graced with illuminated coach lamps and Silver Anniversary script badges. It was powered by the 302 and fitted with the four-speed transmission, and cast aluminum wheels were fitted to the metric TRX tires from Michelin.

The twenty-fifth year of Thunderbird production found the latest iteration wearing a highly angular set of clothing, and was offered in several anniversary variations, including the Heritage edition shown here.

Inside the birthday edition, the driver monitored his travel with the help of an all-electronic instrument array. Cruise control, air-conditioning, and extra-heavy floor carpets were all in place to make this model more comfortable. An electronic keyless entry system was also included in the package. Ford was able to

The 1980 Silver Anniversary Thunderbird
The Proudest Bird of All

The Silver Anniversary Thunderbird grows naturally out of twenty-five years of triumphant Thunderbirds.

In honor of that occasion, we have produced the Silver Anniversary Thunderbird. It is, in a word, a knockout.

Both the inside and the outside are all silver. A silver bird representing the ultimate in Thunderbird's sophisticated automotive design.

Many Thunderbird options are standard. AM-FM stereo, air conditioning, power windows, power brakes, power seats, white sidewalls, power antenna and speed control.

Other options standard on the Silver Anniversary Thunderbird

are: owner's nameplate, digital speedometer, keyless entry system.

Like all 1980 Thunderbirds, it was conceived and produced in a new contemporary size. This size and the new automatic

overdrive transmission which is standard on this car, optional on other Thunderbirds, result in excellent ratings of ⑰ EPA est. MPG—29 est. hwy. MPG.*

If you're looking for a car that expresses you, consider joining the many who find Thunderbird an expression of their individuality. The Silver Anniversary Thunderbird.

Road Test awards Thunderbird "best domestic car for 1980."

*Compare this to other cars. Your mileage may differ depending on speed, weather and trip length. Actual hwy. mileage will be lower than estimates. Calif. ratings lower.

THUNDERBIRD

FORD DIVISION ⟨Ford⟩

sell quite a few copies of the anniversary Bird, even with a list price of $11,679. The car buyer of the 1980s proved to be toy-happy, and this model seemed to offer the perfect combination.

But the price of the basic Thunderbird had risen by $500 despite the elimination of many options in the latest version. These prices, as well as the unrest of the world economy, did nothing to help Thunderbird sales, and fewer than 157,000 were built. This drastic drop in sales indicated that the latest iteration of the classic Thunderbird was not the greatest.

1981:
The Six-Cylinder Birds

IF THE MANAGEMENT AT FORD had been disappointed by sales in 1980, 1981 would not help to restore their faith in the Thunderbird. Inflation continued to ravage the economy, and the U.S. consumer was paying more than ever for less than before. Prices of the Thunderbird line expanded by more than $1,000 per copy and contributed to the downward slope of sales.

The actual design of the '81 saw little change from the previous year, with the exception of mild alterations at both

ends. The front grille was no longer visible beneath the front bumper, and the taillight array was trimmed with a pair of larger T-Bird emblems.

In Ford's effort to justify the large cost increase, many items that were previously offered as options were now incorporated into the basic Thunderbird trim package. Halogen headlights, vinyl body-side trim, a remote left-side mirror, and the front bench seat were among the new standard equipment.

The Town Landau model remained the middle-of-the-road trim package and was equipped with a raft of additional features. Inside the Landau was a tilt steering wheel, AM/FM radio, and interval wipers. Outside were dual remote mirrors, wire wheel covers, and whitewall tires. The padded half-roof was offered in several colors and added a touch of distinction to the Landau. Selling for a list price of $8,689, it was still not the priciest Bird on the floor.

For those who wanted their Thunderbirds to be miniature luxury vehicles, the Heritage was an enticing choice. At a cost of more than $11,000, it was certainly priced as a luxury car and offered a lengthy list of standard equipment.

Along with all of the features of the Landau, the Heritage had a thickly padded half-roof that was augmented by a satin aluminum strap, which wrapped around the leading edge. The hood ornament sparkled with the look of cut crystal, adding another touch of elegance. The interior was also outfitted with numerous upgrades, including optional leather seating.

The most radical departure from Thunderbirds of years gone by was the fitting of a standard six-cylinder engine. First seen in the 1980 models, the inline six displaced 3.3 liters and pumped out 200 horsepower. Thunderbird loyalists were appalled by this alteration, but many prospecive buyers welcomed the higher level of fuel economy that the smaller engine offered.

For dyed-in-the-wool T-Bird enthusiasts, optional engines were offered in both 4.2- and 5.0-liter V8 configurations. With the cost of fuel rising on a daily basis, only 83 percent of the 1981s were ordered with the thirstier V8 motors.

ABOVE, LEFT: Sales literature for the 1980 Silver edition Thunderbird proclaimed it to be "The Proudest Bird of All," but many enthusiasts would question the rhetoric. The price of the Bird had risen significantly, while the list of available options had grown smaller.

Production numbers for 1981 totaled about half what they had been the previous year, but rumors of a radical new Bird kept dreams alive for Thunderbird enthusiasts.

1982:
The Lull Before the Storm

THE BIRD MARKET WAS ONCE again ripe for a new design. Thus, changes to the 1982 Birds were kept to a minimum, as the stage was being set for the arrival of the all-new 1983s. Three trim levels were still offered, and each was equipped with more toys than the one below it. Prices continued their escalation, but the economy had yet to settle into any predictable trend.

Engine options for the Thunderbird were more limited for the new models and were largely based on the inline-six variations. Both the base model and the Landau came standard with 3.3-liter motivation, while a 3.8-liter example was made available at extra cost. The upscale Heritage was driven by the 3.8, but could also be fitted with a 4.2-liter V8 for an additional fee. With fuel economy still fresh on everyone's mind, only about 61 percent of the '82s were driven by the hungrier motor. This figure was down more than 20 percent

> **ABOVE:** Overall changes for the 1981 Birds were minimal, despite the six-cylinder engine beneath the hood.

over the previous models; this would remain the trend for several years as people tried to squeeze more mileage from every gallon of costly fuel.

Transmission options were limited, but the three-speed Selectshift that was standard in the base and Landau models could be supplanted by the four-speed automatic overdrive variant for an additional fee. The four-speed trans was standard in the well-equipped Heritage and, when mated with the V8, it delivered a slight improvement in the mpg ratings. A larger, 21-gallon (79L) fuel tank allowed more distance between fill-ups.

Compared with years past, the color options seemed minimal. The buyer had a choice of only eleven standard exterior colors, along with three extra-cost Metallic Glow shades. Interior options were dizzying, with a total of eighty-six different combinations of colors, fabrics, and seating configurations. The cockpit was complete with a Tripminder computer that allowed the driver to monitor a multitude of functions while on the road.

If sales of the 1981 models had been a disappointment, the 1982s must have caused several bouts of insomnia among the management teams at Ford, barely exceeding 45,000 units for the model year. Ford was more than anxious to roll out the all-new 1983s and return, hopefully, to the glory days of the sporty Thunderbird.

CHAPTER FOUR

THE AERO BIRDS TAKE OFF

WITH A YEAR of dismal sales behind them, the new Thunderbirds had nowhere to go but up. The preceding design had begun to alienate nearly every segment of the market, and a different tack was taken with the 1983 models.

1983–1986: The First Aero Birds

THE KEY WORD FOR FORD in the 1980s was aerodynamics. Although the Ford Taurus is often credited as the trailblazer in aerodynamic design, the 1983 Thunderbird first displayed the sleek, smooth styling a full three years before the Taurus appeared. Both cars, designed by Jack Telnack (who had also been responsible for the Mustang fastback in 1965), sported a sculpted, rounded design that reduced wind resistance. Ford once again broke new ground, and the rest of the automotive industry scurried behind, trying to replicate the successful new design.

1983:
The Arrival of the Aero Birds

ALTHOUGH IT WAS NOT WELCOMED universally, the '83 was a radical departure from any previous Bird and proved to be a hot seller.

The all-new aerodynamic look was achieved by scrapping every square inch of the last T-Bird and giving the overall dimensions a trimmer package. The 1983

PAGES 78–79: The rounded profile of the mid-'80s Thunderbird was a sign of things to come at Ford. A few years after the "Aero Bird" debuted, Ford's new Taurus took the smooth shape to the next level, and took the market by storm. RIGHT: The 1983 Birds were slick and stealthy: the grille and fenders were smoothly sculpted, and the rear end was tapered and deeply sloped. INSET: Interiors on the '83 Thunderbirds were places of form and function, with little excess trim.

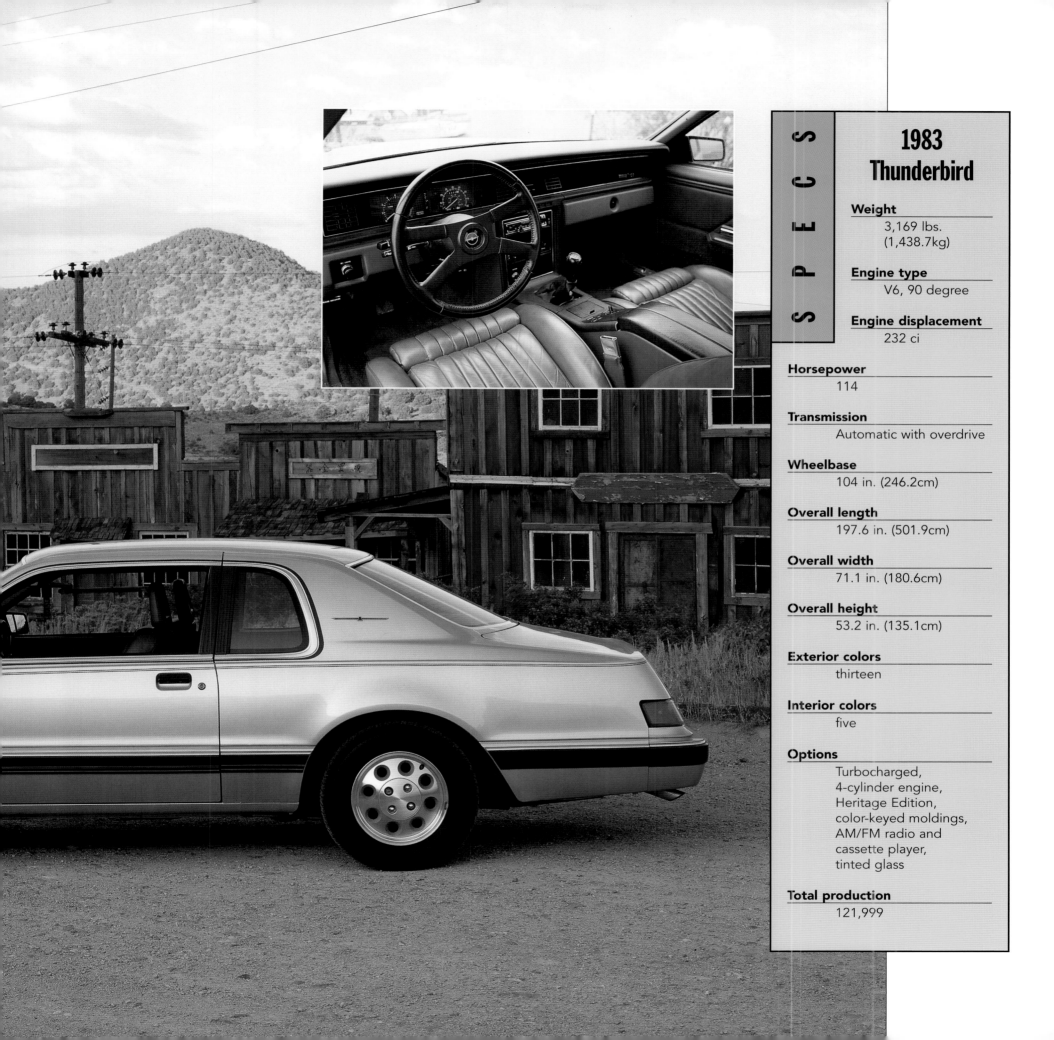

S P E C S

1983
Thunderbird

Weight
3,169 lbs.
(1,438.7kg)

Engine type
V6, 90 degree

Engine displacement
232 ci

Horsepower
114

Transmission
Automatic with overdrive

Wheelbase
104 in. (246.2cm)

Overall length
197.6 in. (501.9cm)

Overall width
71.1 in. (180.6cm)

Overall height
53.2 in. (135.1cm)

Exterior colors
thirteen

Interior colors
five

Options
Turbocharged,
4-cylinder engine,
Heritage Edition,
color-keyed moldings,
AM/FM radio and
cassette player,
tinted glass

Total production
121,999

Who Put the Aero in the Aero Birds?

Born in Ford Hospital and raised in Detroit—his father was a Ford autoworker—Jack Telnack seems to have been bred to work for Ford. After earning a degree in industrial design, he headed back to Detroit to do just that. In almost forty years at Ford, he reshaped the American automobile, and every stroke of his pen has left an indelible mark in automotive history. His earlier projects included the 1961 Galaxie and the 1972 Fiesta, and he played a major role in the redesign of the 1979 Mustang. By 1980, Telnack was Ford's Chief Design Executive.

The garish, and overly ornate trim and boxy shape of the early-'80s Birds conflicted with Telnack's clean, contemporary vision, and Telnack's team set about creating a ground-up, groundbreaking redesign. The result—a smooth, rounded shape that sliced a clean profile in the wind tunnel—set the auto industry on its ear.

Despite the smooth, wind-cheating silhouette, the new Bird's curvy form met with less-than-glowing reviews in the media. Yet consumers loved the fresh look, sensing something of a return to the sporting nature of the T-Birds of old. As Telnack's new Bird sold in record numbers, he set his sights on a new project that took the aesthetic sense and aerodynamic styling of the Bird to the next level. In 1986, Telnack's new Taurus hit the market, and rewrote the book for automotive design.

Thunderbird was 3 inches (7.5cm) shorter and 3 inches (7.5cm) narrower than the '82. The wheelbase was reduced by nearly 3 inches as well, but inside there was actually more room. The slippery bodywork had a drag coefficient of only .35, which was far better than the boxy shape of the previous variants. This new design direction was highly appealing to younger drivers, though it left some dyed-in-the-wool Thunderbird fans cold.

The Aero Birds came in three flavors for 1983. The line-up consisted of the base model, the Heritage, and the exciting new Turbo Coupe. While they shared bodywork and most running gear, the three variations were distinct. All three models provided the driver and front-seat passenger with more head and leg room, but anyone seated in the back had fewer cubic inches available to them. The trunk was also slightly smaller, and 3 fewer gallons (11L) of fuel could be carried in the tank.

The base model came with a 232-cubic-inch V6 engine that produced 114 horsepower and 175 foot-pounds of torque. An optional V8 motor, which displaced 302 cubic inches, could be ordered. While delivering 130 horsepower and 240 foot-pounds of torque, the V8 was selected by only about 31 percent of buyers in 1983. Many people were still carrying scars from the recent oil shortage and were not yet willing to jump into a gas-guzzling vehicle.

The Turbo Coupe was outfitted with a 2.3-liter four-cylinder engine that was boosted by a turbocharger to a rating of 145 horsepower. This combination provided plenty of power while still maintaining a decent mpg reading. Despite this unique packaging, less than 11 percent of the 1983 Birds were delivered in this trim.

Even with a certain percentage of the marketplace complaining about the new Thunderbird design, it sold very well. Just under 122,000 copies were snapped up, a figure nearly triple that of the 1982 models.

LEFT: Offered as a total package, the 1984 Fila coupe was delivered in a two-tone color scheme, complete with accompanying appointments, such as leather seats and coordinated aluminum wheels.
INSET: A slender, yet recognizable, Thunderbird logo was found on each of the rectangular taillight lenses.

1984:
Aero Birds Continue
to Soar

AFTER LOGGING A ROBUST YEAR of sales in 1983, the Thunderbird was back on the fast track. The proven success of the new shape prompted the Ford design team to leave well enough alone and make only minor cosmetic alterationsfor 1984. There were a few changes within the ranks in an effort to sell even more Thunderbirds in the current model year.

Although the body went largely unchanged, electronic fuel injection (EFI) was added to the entire range of engines. The Turbo Coupe's four-cylinder power plant could be mated to an automatic transmission, which bumped total sales of the automatic T-Birds to 93 percent of all built for the year. A larger fuel tank was also fitted to deliver longer range from every fill-up.

The model lineup saw a mild shift, as the Heritage became the Élan and a new entrant was offered alongside the other three. The Fila package was designed in conjunction with the sporting goods company of the same name, and the Thunderbird was trimmed in fitting fashion. It was dipped in an exclusive white paint and devoid of almost all the usual bright trim. Special striping also helped to differentiate the Fila from the other variants. Inside the new model, the front bucket seats could be ordered in white leather or gray cloth, both of which were specific to this trim level. The Fila could be purchased with a 3.8-liter V6 or with the more potent 5.0-liter V8 for an additional fee. Interior packages continued to abound, and a total of thirty-two different combinations were available to the discriminating buyer. Eight exterior colors were also shown for the year.

LEFT: Ford celebrated the thirtieth anniversary of the venerable Thunderbird in 1985. Few changes were made to the car that year, the most obvious of which was the new Thunderbird logo—a feathered bird replaced the old geometric design. PAGES 88–89: The Thunderbird ruled the NASCAR circuit in the mid-1980s, with Bill Elliott driving his Aero Bird to record-setting victories. His Number 9 Coors Thunderbird scorched the pavement to an all-time NASCAR lap record of 212.809 mph (342.410kph) at Talladega in 1987.

All in all, it was a very good year for the latest Bird, with sales reaching nearly 171,000, an increase of almost 50,000 over the previous year.

1985:
Another Anniversary

THE 1985 MODEL YEAR MARKED the thirtieth year of production for the Thunderbird, and the name proved to be a resilient competitor among the growing ranks of players in the field.

Once again, the basic body went unchanged, with a minimum of visible outward trim modifications. A new Thunderbird logo—a feathered bird instead of the old geometric design—was grafted onto the usual locations and would be about the only way to discern the 1985 model from previous years. The same four variations were offered, each benefiting from minor upgrades.

The thirtieth-anniversary model was trimmed in an exclusive paint and trim scheme and adorned with commemorative badges. The other Thunderbird models were sold in one of fourteen exterior colors. Half these shades were of the standard variety; the other half were extra-cost Clearcoat tones. The interior came complete with a

new instrument panel that included a digital speedometer and complementary analog gauges. Thirty-three variations of trim and seating were available to complicate the buying process.

In the motivation department, an all-new five-speed manual transmission was offered, but only 8 percent of buyers selected this option. The 2.3-liter turbo engine was fitted with an electronic boost control and found an additional 13 horses (for a total of 157 horsepower) onboard.

On the racing circuit, the Thunderbird was racking up an impressive tally of first-place finishes. But even the adage "Win on Sunday, sell on Monday" was not enough to push sales beyond that of the previous year, and production actually slipped by nearly 20,000 units for 1985.

1986:
Slight Changes, Big Wins

THE DOMINATION OF FORD'S THUNDERBIRDS on the NASCAR circuit continued in 1986, and their on-track victories drew an ever larger audience into the showrooms.

The 1986 model saw little in the way of alterations but was trimmed with more electronics as the high-tech era dawned. New federal mandates were the reason for the appearance of the high-mounted third brake light, a change seen on all cars built for U.S. consumption. Under the hood, the earlier manual prop rod had been replaced with sprung hinges, making it safer and more convenient to do routine maintenance.

The Fila trim level was removed from the catalog because of a lack of consumer interest. Three variations remained, doing their best to fill the needs of buyers. The base model started at $11,452, the Élan at $12,554, and the racy Turbo Coupe at $14,143. Optional trim and engine choices added to these prices, and few were sold as base models.

Electronic enhancements included a new climate-control system, and even the lowly base T-Bird came complete with an electronically tuned AM/FM radio. In all but the Turbo Coupe, the inclusion of wood-tone materials to the interiors added a touch of elegance. The base and Élan versions were offered in five standard colors or finished in one of eight optional Clearcoat tints. The Turbo was available in three standard shades with five Clearcoat options. There was also a variety of two-tone combinations available as well as a selection of complementary pinstripe packages.

Under the hood, the 3.8-liter V6 returned as the standard engine, with the 5.0-liter V8 as an option.

OPPOSITE: For 1986, little was changed on the popular Aero Birds, as sales continued to grow at a brisk pace and designers busied themselves with the upcoming 1987 revision.

New hydraulic engine mounts helped to smooth out any vibrations that might otherwise reach the occupants.

Although little had changed from the previous year, sales expanded at a rapid pace. Just under 164,000 Thunderbirds were produced, 19 percent of which had the V8 option; another 13 percent were driven by the turbo-charged four-cylinder motor.

1987:
All-New Skin
for the Aero Bird

ALTHOUGH THE PROFILE OF THE 1987 Thunderbird was highly similar to the last edition, it did not share a single inch of sheet metal with the 1986 models. The overall design was sleeker and featured flush-mounted side glass in an effort to enhance the car's ability to slip through the air without a fuss. Both the front and back ends were also revised and took on a decidedly more contemporary look. The Turbo Coupe sported treatments at both ends that were exclusive to that model. In contrast to most product cycles, 1987 was the first of only two years for this variation on the Thunderbird theme.

The Thunderbird nest comprised four different models for 1987. In addition to the return of the base and Turbo Coupe, there were the two new Thunderbird models: the LX and the Sport.

T-Birds on the Track

The all-new aerodynamic shape of the 1983 Thunderbird did not go unnoticed by builders of racing machines. The new Birds weren't just selling well—they were raising eyebrows on the NASCAR circuit, where several major teams were taking the slippery new shape for a ride out on the track, with some very positive results.

Dale Earnhardt, Bill Elliott, and Buddy Baker were quick to hop behind the wheel of the latest Thunderbird. After getting some early bugs worked out, the NASCAR spec Birds began to rack up some impressive wins in the 1983 season. The Firecracker 400 in Daytona, Winston Western 500, Nashville, and

Talladega all saw the Thunderbird rolling into the winner's circle.

The winning streak continued in 1984 on the oval tracks of the NASCAR circuit, and Bob Glidden used the ultra-smooth design to capture a number of wins in the pro-stock class as well. As development continued, Bill Elliott took his Thunderbird to eleven victories in the Winston Cup series in 1985. Never before had a single driver won as many races in a single season.

Changes in the NASCAR rules for 1986 took some of the wind out of the Thunderbird's wings, but the Birds continued to take the checkered flag in many a race during the years to follow.

Bill Elliott
MELLING
AUTOMOTIVE PRODUCTS
Coors
9
Motorcraft
QUALITY PARTS

The new LX was powered by the same 3.8-liter V6 as the base model but was assembled with a set of accent stripes and styled wheels to set it apart. The Sport was driven by a standard 5.0-liter V8 engine as well as a raft of appropriate styling clues. The Turbo Coupe was made more powerful by the addition of an intercooler to the potent 2.3-liter, four-cylinder motor. The functional hood scoops helped to funnel fresh air into the intercooler, boosting horsepower to 190. The Turbo was also fitted with a set of four 16- by 7-inch (41 by 18cm) cast aluminum wheels, which were not available on any other Thunderbird that year. All four versions of the Thunderbird were slowed by brakes that included an antilock system as well as a ride control package that really improved handling.

Color choices for the Thunderbirds were shifting toward the optional Clearcoat shades, and a record nine were offered for 1987. Only four standard colors were shown for the base and LX models. The Turbo was available in combinations of two standard or six Clearcoat hues.

The changes in the new Bird won it high praise from much of the motoring press, and it continued to do well on the NASCAR circuit. Winning races and the minds of the media failed to capture consumers' hearts, however, and sales slid to just over 128,000 units for the year. It seemed that nearly constant change was required to hold the attention of the fickle buying public, but Detroit had changed its production methods, and radical year-to-year alterations were no longer cost-effective. The growing ranks of the competition were not helping the Thunderbird either, but the consumer was the ultimate winner as the car companies battled for a slice of the pie.

The entire front end of the Thunderbird was redesigned for 1987. A lower, wider grille was incorporated, and the old quad sealed headlamps were replaced with new halogen lights.

1988:
The Winning Ways Continue

IN 1988, THE second and final year for this variation of the Thunderbird, few changes were evident. The same four models made up the Thunderbird team, but each was given minor refinements.

A 3.8-liter V6 engine remained the standard power plant on the base and LX models, but it operated more smoothly with the addition of a balancing shaft. The fuel injection system was also upgraded to the multipoint variety, which helped the new V6 produce an additional 20 horses. Anyone interested in extra horsepower could order a base or LX with the 5.0-liter V8 engine. The V8 exhaled through a dual exhaust system, which added 5 horses to the usual output.

Delivered with the 5.0-liter V8 as the standard motor, the Sport also breathed through the new dual exhaust system. Inside, new articulated front seats helped to convey the sporting nature of the model. The previous Sport had an array of electronic gauges, but the '88 informed the driver via analog instrumentation. Further exclusive trim pieces helped to separate the Sport from other T-Birds.

About the only change for the Turbo Coupe was the price, which increased by nearly $500. Still powered by an intercooled, turbocharged four-cylinder engine, this model remained popular with the racing enthusiasts. Other carryover features were the five-speed transmission, antilock brakes, and electronic ride control. Sixteen-inch (41cm) alloy wheels dressed up the Turbo.

The base, LX, Sport, and Turbo Coupe were all offered with their own sets of color options, as were several two-tone combinations, along with coordinating striping to accent the chosen body color. All models except the base could be ordered with a leather-trimmed interior. Electric sunroofs were still available, but they were not purchased in huge numbers. Of the total production figures, 25 percent were of the turbo variety and 28 percent V8-powered, with the balance using the amiable V6. Although little had changed from the 1987 models, sales increased by almost 20,000 units, bringing the total to 147,243 for the 1986 model year.

Part of the Thunderbird's commercial success could be attributed to NASCAR racer Bill Elliott piloting his Thunderbird to the top spot in the Winston Cup circuit in the 1988 season. The next design for the Thunderbird arrived in 1989, and both the public and the racing world waited with great anticipation to see if the domination would continue.

CHAPTER FIVE

THE TWILIGHT OF THE T-BIRD

1989–1993: **Sweeping Changes**

THE MANAGEMENT AT FORD HAD LONG SINCE demonstrated a desire to keep the Thunderbird name alive, so it came as no surprise when the decision was made to devote special attention to the eleventh-generation Birds.

More than $1 billion was earmarked for the redesign of the '89s, and the final result showcased Ford's efforts in every way.

1989:
A New Bird Swoops In

THE 1989 THUNDERBIRDS WORE A fresh new coat of sheet metal and rode on a wheelbase 9 inches (23cm) shorter than its predecessor. The overall length had been shortened by just less than 4 inches (10cm), and height was reduced by 1 inch (2.5cm). Actual width had been boosted by almost 2 inches (5cm), and these new characteristics provided much-needed room in the interior of the Turbo Coupe.

The base model (priced at $14,612) and LX ($16,817) were still powered by the time-tested 3.8-liter V6, but other improvements were found underneath their svelte new skins. Four-wheel independent suspension was a Thunderbird first and provided an extra measure of comfort and handling to the driver and passengers. The steering was still of the rack-and-pinion variety, but a speed-sensitive variable assist was in place to enhance the feel of the car regardless of speed.

However, one dark spot on the new T-Bird was its weight. The new models carried 300 to 500 extra pounds (136 to 227kg) of baggage over the previous examples. Although not the end of the world, it did play a part in higher fuel consumption and a reduction in speed.

The LX trim level came complete with a full complement of standard amenities. A power driver seat was joined by power door locks, power mirrors, and cruise control. A set of electronic gauges kept the driver informed.

As exciting as these new models were, there was one star that shone even brighter. The Sport model was no longer a part of the Thunderbird offerings, but the new Super Coupe, which replaced the Turbo Coupe, overshadowed

this loss. Dubbed SC for short, the new car was powered by a supercharged V6 engine that pumped out 215 horsepower with prodigious amounts of torque. An intercooler played a supporting role by keeping the rush of incoming oxygen cool. Due to an early problem with the crankshafts, the SC's release was delayed, causing a huge backlog of orders.

The bodywork was the same as on the other models, but the $19,823 SC was given several styling cues to set it apart from its brethren. The initials *SC* were molded into both the front and rear fasciae, and aerodynamic body trim gave the SC a purposeful look. The front air dam was also fitted with a pair of high-intensity fog lamps to aid the driver in less-than-perfect weather.

Underneath the SC bodywork, a handling suspension package was onboard that included beefy antisway bars and refined components. Four-wheel disc brakes were aided by an antilock system to keep things under control in the worst of conditions.

Inside, articulated sport seats and an analog dash completed the performance package. Leather was available for those

PAGES 92–93: Turbo Coupes were supplanted by the new SC, or Super Coupe, in 1989. The SC was equipped with a supercharged V6 that produced 215hp. The chrome logo seemed to be spreading its wings on the latest version of the Thunderbird, which was fitting, considering the level of power on tap. BELOW AND OPPOSITE: Sexy alloy wheels helped to set the 1989 SC apart from the other Thunderbirds. Along with the powerful supercharged engine, the SC was fitted with aerodynamic trim pieces that made the Bird look fast, even when it was quietly parked.

who wished to add a touch of luxury to this otherwise pure sports coupe.

With such a huge investment behind the car, Ford obviously hoped for record sales of the latest Bird. But the final tally for the model year was down by more than 32,000 units, because of both the delay in getting the SC out and the higher prices of the vehicles themselves. Although the T-Bird was capable of outrunning some of the German offerings, consumers were beginning to balk at the sticker prices, especially on the SC. Only time would tell if Ford had invested its money wisely.

1990:
Another Birthday

AN ALL-NEW THUNDERBIRD WAS introduced in 1989, so it made sense that the 1990 models would receive only minor alterations. This marked the thirty-fifth year of production for the Bird, but most of the hullabaloo had occurred in the previous year.

The base, LX, and Super Coupe models remained in the catalog for 1990, but a growing list of options was being offered to increase buyers' selections. A new wrinkle for many Detroit car builders was the bundling of options at a reduced cost. This may have limited the individual flavor of each Thunderbird assembled, but it saved both Ford and the consumer some serious cash.

The Power Equipment Group and Luxury Group were available on the base and LX models. The Power Equipment Group added electric door locks, an electrically adjusted driver seat, and a remote release for both the trunk and fuel-filler door. The Luxury Group went one step further and added cruise control, tilt steering wheel, power outside mirrors, and additional courtesy lights.

In addition to these groups of options, a few individual choices remained. Cast alloy wheels, an antitheft system, a CD player, and a Ford/JBL sound system were all available as individual upgrades.

As in anniversary years of the past, a special edition of the Thunderbird was offered. The thirty-fifth birthday was marked by the January 1990 release of an anniversary-edition SC. Mechanically unchanged from the standard SC, this edition was adorned with special cosmetic trim to set it apart. Special black and titanium paint was highlighted by blue accent stripes. The alloy wheels were also done in

black, and commemorative badges were found both inside and out. The interior was trimmed in suede and leather and featured a split rear seat that folded down for additional trunk space. All of this special trim came with a price tag nearly $2,000 more than the base price of $20,394, and only 5,000 copies of the anniversary Bird were built.

Total output of the '90 Thunderbirds slipped to 113,957 units for the model year, and industry watchers were beginning to wonder how long Ford would keep the car in the lineup.

OPPOSITE: Alongside the SC, the LX version shown offered a higher level of luxury for the buyer in search of more show than go for the '91 model year. BELOW: With a front fascia that mimicked the nares of an eagle, the Supercharged Coupe took an even more aggressive stance than before. PAGES 98–99: In 1989, the Thunderbird Super Coupe replaced the old Sport model. The new SC was powered by a supercharged V6 engine that pumped out 215 horsepower.

1991:
The V8 Rides Again

IN 1991, THE AUTOMOTIVE INDUSTRY was in a bit of a slump, and Ford was not immune. With sales of the Thunderbird dropping like a stone in 1990, Ford was not about to invest enormous amounts of cash in the line. It stood to reason that the '91 Birds were almost identical to the 1990 models.

About the only news worth reporting was the return of the V8 motor option. Thunderbird buyers had been missing the extra power that the bigger motor supplied, but

Thunderbird Fan Clubs

With a history that spans more than forty years, the Thunderbird has a following that is tough to beat. Owners' clubs can be found throughout the world, and if you live in the United States, chances are that on any given weekend, you'll be able to find at least one gathering of T-bird aficionados in your region. Some clubs focus on a single era or generation of the Bird, while others accept any Thunderbird ever built. While the early models remain among the most popular periods, late-model Birds enjoy a following that is every bit as dedicated as that of the classic '57s.

Joining a Thunderbird club is one of the easiest ways to increase the pleasure of owning and driving your Bird, and a great way to keep in contact with other owners for advice, parts exchanges, and tips on repair and performance. An enormous quantity of parts, both original and remanufactured, can be found through the clubs, making it possible to build a 1955 Thunderbird entirely from spare parts. So if you're looking for a T-Bird, and can't wait until 2000 to get one, find a used one, join a club, and start restoring!

S P E C S

1990
Thunderbird

Weight
3,267 lbs.
(1,483,2kg)

Engine type
V6, 90 degree,
OHV

Engine displacement
232 ci

Horsepower
140

Transmission
Four-speed automatic

Wheelbase
113 in. (287.0cm)

Overall length
198.7 in. (504.7cm)

Overall width
72.7 in. (184.7cm)

Overall height
52.7 in. (133.9cm)

Exterior colors
eleven

Interior colors
four

Options
SC model with super-
charged engine,
35th Anniversary edition,
rear window defroster,
antitheft system,
CD player

Total production
113,957

PAGES 100–101: With another anniversary in 1990, Ford dipped the Bird in black, then added a few touches of silver to commemorate the occasion. This is the original prototype for the Thirty-fifth Anniversary edition SC. RIGHT: An optional five-liter, high-output engine was slipped under the hood of the 1991 T-Bird for those who preferred to have their power deliverd the old-fashioned way.

Ford had no immediate plans for an engine that would fit. The Mustang was propelled by a healthy 225-horsepower V8, but size differences made the swap less than perfect. Engineers at Ford were able to shoe-horn a Mustang 5.0 into the '91 Thunderbird but found it was too high for the hood to close. Several experiments were made with a bulging hood to clear the motor, but this voided the clean lines of the design, and the idea was scrapped.

By altering the intake manifold and some other hardware on the existing Mustang engine, the engineers finally got it to fit within the close quarters of the Thunderbird's new engine bay. These changes dropped the horsepower to 200 but at least gave Bird buyers back their beloved V8. The optional V8 motor would cost the consumer an extra $1,100, but sales of this variant still managed to account for 21 percent of all Birds built for 1991. The extra V8 sales took a serious bite out of the Super Coupe sales, numbers that plunged to just below 5 percent of all Thunderbirds sold for the year.

An increasing number of features appeared on both the base and LX models. In an effort to justify the price increases, the list of standard equipment grew quickly. Included in the price of the base coupe were a rear window defogger, deluxe wheel covers, air-conditioning, tinted glass, and power windows and steering, as well as several other items that had been extra-cost options.

The LX added to the list with illuminated entry, illuminated visor mirrors, reclining "luxury" cloth bucket seats, an armrest, a leather-wrapped tilt steering wheel, power door locks, and cruise control. When ordered with the V8 engine, the LX made for a highly confident, comfortable machine, even though it was tough to distinguish between it and a base-level Bird.

The SC was back, but sales faltered alarmingly. The V8 engine was greatly preferred over the more costly supercharged V6, and a well-equipped LX was considered to be a far better value.

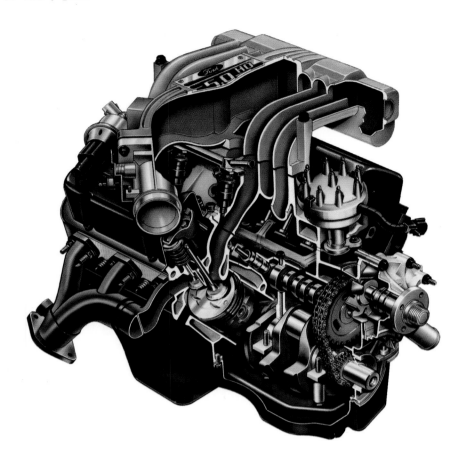

The anemic automotive marketplace was claiming many victims, and the Thunderbird found itself swept up in the muck. Only 82,973 Thunderbirds were assembled in 1991, and the future was growing ever darker for the legendary car.

1992:
The Slump Continues

THE THUNDERBIRD WAS A RARITY in 1992 since it was still running on a rear-wheel-drive platform. The vast majority of its competition had switched over to the more modern front-wheel-drive layout, putting the T-Bird at an even bigger disadvantage.

There were four models of the Thunderbird in the 1992 brochures and, as usual, each one had a slightly different slant on the same theme. The Sport Coupe and LX models touted a front fascia like the Super Coupe but were devoid of the SC stamping. The Sport Coupe rolled on a set of alloy wheels and added a leather-wrapped steering wheel to its list of standard equipment. All four variants were slowed by disc brakes at every corner of the chassis, bringing a new level of confidence to the driver.

Motivation was still provided by the 140-horsepower V6 or the 200-horsepower V8. The Super Coupe was still the only way to get the supercharged V6 under the hood of a Bird. As sales declined, so did the interest in the V8 power plant. Birds delivered with this option in 1992 dropped 4 percent, while the SC's sales increased slightly for the model year.

For the first time, there were no manual transmissions offered in the Thunderbird lineup in 1992, a direct reaction to a lack of consumer interest. People were becoming spoiled by smoother and more efficient automatic transmissions, and those who preferred the hands-on feel purchased vehicles more suited to the effort.

BELOW: The smooth sheetmetal and flush-mounted side glass helped to guide the 1992 Thunderbird through the atmosphere with ease.

For the standard, Sport Coupe, and LX models, there were eleven available colors, four of which were new for 1992. The Super Coupe was offered in five exterior shades, with

four interior themes to choose from. A power sunroof was still an option, but it was selected by only about 12 percent of buyers.

Despite the lagging sales in the showrooms, the Thunderbird continued its dominance on racing circuits around the country. Both the NASCAR and ARCA series found Thunderbirds in the winner's circle often.

Ford's diminishing interest in changing the Thunderbird was reflected in production. Only 77,789 units were built to fill orders in 1992, and there were no plans for a radical makeover in the foreseeable future.

1993:
Streamlining the Flock

WITH SALES OF THE THUNDERBIRD on a slippery downward slope, Ford needed to implement some changes before pulling the plug completely. Rather than redesigning the Bird from the ground up, Ford determined that the best strategy was to take the existing car and make it a better value.

The 1993 models were virtually unchanged from the previous year, but a new pricing structure made them far more attractive. With research and development costs already amortized, all Ford needed to do was streamline the offerings.

For 1993, Ford offered only two Thunderbird models. Gone were the standard model and the Sport Coupe, leaving behind the LX and Super Coupe. By "value pricing" each of these remaining versions, Ford hoped to bring more buyers back into the showrooms. The 1993 LX's window sticker was nearly $3,000 less than that of the previous year, and the car itself actually had a few minor improvements. Although this did nothing for the resale value of '92 models, it increased popularity of the Bird radically. The SC was also given several slight upgrades, but its price fell by only $16 for the new year.

The LX was delivered with the 140-horsepower V6 coupled with the four-speed automatic overdrive transmission. The bigger V8 was still offered as an option and was fed with EFI. Inside the '93 LX, luxury upholstery, door trim, and carpeting brought a higher level of comfort to the buyer. A pair of bucket seats and a full-length console rounded out the newest level of Thunderbird trim.

The LX could be had in one of ten exterior colors, with four choices for the interior. There would be several changes in the color charts before the end of the model year, causing a few of the shades to become collectibles.

The SC was back with its 210-horsepower, supercharged V6 engine. A boost gauge helped keep the driver informed of the pressure being delivered, but the seat-of-the-pants acceleration also made a fine indicator of progress. Along with the higher horsepower, the SC came equipped with a long list of handling tricks. Automatic Ride Control, Handling Package, and Traction-Lok Axle were but a few of the amenities found under the SC's aerobody. Inside, cloth buckets, a light package, and a sport steering wheel added to the perceived value of the $22,030 car.

Colors for the SC bodywork were limited to five on the outside, three on the inside. There were also changes made to the SC color choices during the model year.

Outside the busy showrooms, motorsports activity was booming and did its part to lure customers in to buy the streetbound versions of the racing Birds. Between the suc-

cesses on the racetracks and the new pricing structure, Ford racked up sales nearly double those of the year before. An amazing 122,415 copies of the Thunderbird rolled into customers' driveways, a number that had not been seen since 1988. It seemed that the final nail was not yet ready for the Thunderbird's coffin.

1994–1997: A Nip and Tuck for the Late-'90s Bird

STILL FEELING THAT A MAJOR OVERHAUL would be unprofitable, Ford opted for a face-lift for the 1994 Thunderbird. A fresher, sleeker, more efficient car was the result. Mechanically unchanged, the '94s were simply revised '93 models, tucked and trimmed for a more streamlined look and improved aerodynamics.

1994: More "Aero" for the Bird

A SLEEKER, MORE AERODYNAMIC LOOK marked the 1994 Thunderbird. Both front and rear fasciae received a rounder look, with a pair of "nostrils" cut into the front bumper. The latest Thunderbird logo seemed to float in the smoothly contoured opening in the all-new hood. Airflow for engine cooling was routed through a space beneath the front bumper instead of an actual opening in the hood. A pair of modern halogen headlights completed the makeover, giving the latest Thunderbird its smoothest look ever.

Inside the new Bird, a highly modernized cockpit featured twin pods: one for the driver, one for the front-seat passenger. The console was swept up into the control panel in a single flowing line, and dual air bags were on duty for safety. Dual cup holders were introduced and soon became a staple in American vehicles. The latest CPC-free air-conditioning kept the occupants cool without being an environmental hazard.

The standard engine for the LX was still the 3.8-liter V6, but Ford had a brand-new V8 that could be ordered as an option. The new 4.6-liter modular V8 delivered more

horsepower, yet it did so with higher fuel economy. Final drive was provided via the electronically shifted automatic transmission. Designed to deliver seamless shifts, the new trans did its part in providing more miles per gallon.

The SC's V6 was fitted with an Eaton supercharger, which delivered more horsepower with less noise. The SC could provide 230 horses upon demand, an increase of 20 over the 1992 version. Underneath all this handiwork, Traction Assist could be added to the Thunderbird and was linked to the all-wheel antilock brake system already in place.

Eleven exterior colors could be paired with five interior shades on the LX, while the SC could be finished in seven exterior hues with four cockpit choices.

The newest look for the Thunderbird was provided with only a mild uptick in price, and more than 130,000 were sold. Much like a star, the Thunderbird was still burning brightly—just before going out.

For 1993, the LX model was given a sleek package that mimicked the faster SC.

1995:
Forty Years, No Celebration

IT HAD BEEN FORTY YEARS since the first Bird had captured the hearts of car buyers, but the light at the end of the tunnel was growing dimmer. With a second consecutive NASCAR championship under its belt, Ford hoped to keep the momentum rolling.

Changes to the 1995 T-Birds were few and far between. With heavy alterations the previous year, there was no reason to change the car further. Sales in 1994 had been extremely strong, and once again Ford was looking forward to continuing its good fortune.

Minor modifications to the interior provided a modicum of additional shoulder room, but the basic layout was unaltered. The CD changer, previously mounted in the trunk, was replaced by an optional in-dash unit that was fed one disc at a time. Speed-sensitive power steering was available as an option when taking delivery of a V6-powered Bird, but it was part of the standard equipment list on the V8 and Super Coupe. To help keep your Thunderbird safe, an antitheft alarm system was also available as an option.

List prices had been given a slight boost for 1995, and the LX went for $17,225, while the SC stickered at $22,735.

After two winning years on the NASCAR circuit, Ford began on a less than enthusiastic note for the 1995 season. Chevrolet's newest Monte Carlo was proving itself to be a worthy adversary and was beginning to dominate the series, pushing the Thunderbird out of the limelight for the first time in three years. Early sales reports for the 1995 model year tallied nearly 10,000 fewer than the last year. These two factors, combined with Ford's hesitancy to redesign the Thunderbird, soon led to the final days of glory.

RIGHT: With the end of production in sight, the Thunderbird was little changed for 1995, but became a low-cost leader in the ever-changing market. PAGES 108–109: Late-model Thunderbirds earned an enviable reputation on the NASCAR circuit, thanks in part to the groundbreaking styling of the Aero Birds. This 1996 racer was driven by Ernie Irvan.

1996–1997:
The End Draws Near?

THE FORTIETH YEAR OF PRODUCTION for the fabled Thunderbird was 1995, but the automotive market was changing faster than Ford could keep up.

Long gone were the balky rear-drive competitors. The only cars utilizing the rear-wheel-drive design were full-boat luxury models and sporty vehicles like the Mustang. In addition to the outdated drivetrain, buyers' loyalty was evaporating. The ever-expanding field of competitive cars did nothing to help the aging Bird retain its position in the marketplace.

Thunderbird fame had long since given up hope of ever seeing another "true" Thunderbird, and consumer loyalty in general was becoming a thing of the past. The automotive field was rife with exciting new models, many of which delivered better performance than the Thunderbird for less money. In basic terms, the Thunderbird was failing to offer enough bang for the buck, and people were demanding more than ever for their hard-earned dollars. The management at Ford was not blind to this situation and knew they had a decision to make about the future of the Thunderbird.

The Mercury Cougar had been sharing the Thunderbird's platform for many years and was being sent out to pasture at the end of the 1997 model year. It didn't take a genius to see the path that the Thunderbird would be following. Modern manufacturing techniques, based on efficiency, could not justifiably be used as an entire assembly line to build a single model, even if it was the venerable Thunderbird.

The Thunderbird soldiered on with few changes for 1997, amid rumors of its imminent demise. Sure enough, after forty two consecutive model years, 1998 marked the first year without a new Thunderbird since the first Bird debuted. To this date, only two other cars—the Chevrolet Corvette (the arch-rival of the original Thunderbird) and the Cadillac Eldorado can lay claim to such a long and consistent life span.

RIGHT: With only two years left on its calendar, the Thunderbird was trimmed with some of the sleekest graphics ever.

OPPOSITE: In its final year of production, the Thunderbird was gifted with one of the smoothest cockpit designs on the 1997 market. LEFT: Even the logo was given a fresh look for the final version.

Thunderbird 2000: The Bird Flies Again

RUMORS OF THE REBIRTH OF the Thunderbird began circulating soon after its apparent demise. The T-Bird's sibling, the Cougar was reincarnated for the 1998 model year, and Ford confirmed plans for a new Thunderbird in the spring of 1998.

Following on the success of the two-seat Mazda Miata and the nostalgia-driven Volkswagen Beetle, the new Thunderbird was unveiled as a concept car at the 1998 Detroit Auto Show. After years of complaints that the Thunderbird had drifted too far from its roadster roots—becoming bloated and lethargic in the process—the new Bird set to land for the 2000 model year takes its styling cues from the classic first-generation Birds of 1955–57. The new two-seater promises the best of both worlds, merging classic styling with modern technology and safety features.

The concept car—which Ford promises will be as close to the production model as was the original Thunderbird concept car that debuted in 1954—features an oval egg-crate grille, two large fog lamps set into the front bumper, and an air scoop integrated into the hood. Chrome brightwork highlights the windshield and the trademark porthole windows. Crisp lines running straight back from the headlamps to the taillamps are a modern nod to the early Bird's legendary fins. A removable hard top is accompanied by a standard convertible top that folds down beneath it. Inside, the classic two-tone color combinations of the fifties are reinterpreted in modern materials and finishes. The new rear-wheel Bird will use the same platform as the 2000 Lincoln LS.

Response to the concept car has been phenomenally positive. The automotive press who witnessed the unveiling—usually a fairly cynical and staid bunch when it comes to new models—broke into uncharacteristically thundering applause at the sight of the new Bird. Come 2000, Ford is hoping that Thunderbird loyalists will do the same.

ABOVE: Unveiled at the Detroit Auto Show in January 1999, the 2000 Thunderbird concept car is everything Bird loyalists could have hoped for—a slick roadster inspired by the classic T-Bird of 1957. OPPOSITE: The last of the old Birds came out in 1997.

T-BIRD CLUBS

INTERNATIONAL CLUBS

Classic Thunderbird Club International   1955–57
1308 E. 29th Street
Signal Hill, CA 90806

International Thunderbird Club   All years
20 Northview Drive
Hanover, PA 17331-4521

Vintage Thunderbird Club International   1958–97
P.O. Box 2250
Dearborn, MI 48123

UNITED STATES
NATIONAL & REGIONAL CLUBS

Heartland Vintage Thunderbird Club of America
1958–69
5002 Gardner
Kansas City, MO 64120
National

New England's Vintage Thunderbird Club   1955–97
170 Pheasant Lane
Manchester, NH 03109
Regional

Northern California Vintage Thunderbird Club of America
1958–66
124 Hollyhock Court
Hercules, CA 94547
Regional

ARIZONA

Arizona Classic Thunderbird Club   1955–57
P.O. Box 5008
Carefree, Arizona 85377

CALIFORNIA

Bay Area Thunderbird Owners Club   1955–57
60 Ridgewood Drive, San Rafael, CA 94901-1130
Local, 1955-1957 Thunderbirds
Chapter #4, Classic Thunderbird Club International

Classic Thunderbird Club of Southern California
1955–57
P.O. Box 1776
West Covina, CA 91793-1776
Chapter #52, Classic Thunderbird Club International

Classic Thunderbirds of San Diego   1955–57
P.O. Box 82844
San Diego, CA 92138
Chapter #24, Classic Thunderbird Club International

Earlybirds of Southern California   1955–57
33821 Colegio Drive
Dana Point, CA 92629
Chapter #7, Classic Thunderbird Club International

Funbirds of Southern California   1958–97
6521 E. Mantova St.
Long Beach, CA 90815
Affiliated with Vintage Thunderbird Club International

Golden Gate Classic Thunderbird Club   1955–57
For more information contact Rita Press, President at
510-799-0556, or E-mail mjprgp@hotcoco.infi.net,
or Rich Lunardi, Vice President at 650-571-8335,
or E-mail lunardi.rich@cnf.com.

Monterey Bay Classic Thunderbird Club   1955–66
546 Cuesta Dr.
Aptos, CA. 95003

Sacramento Classic Thunderbird Club   1955–57
Contact: Chuck Hills at 916-961-1668
Chapter #14, Classic Thunderbird Club International

Santa Clara Valley Thunderbirds   1955–57
P.O. Box 26116
San Jose, CA 94547
Chapter #50, Classic Thunderbird Club International

Sequoia Classic Thunderbird Club.   1955–57
10825 9 1/8 th Ave.
Hanford, CA 93230
Chapter #109, Classic Thunderbird Club International

Thunderbird Circle Club of Orange County   1955–57
17522 Pine Circle
Yorba Linda, CA 92686
Chapter #78, Classic Thunderbird Club International

Thunderbirds of San Diego.   All years
252 Via Villena
Encinitas, CA 92024

Thunderbirds of Sonoma   1955–57
590 Carmody Road
Petaluma, CA 95452
Chapter #33 of the Classic Thunderbird Club International

Valley Classic Thunderbird Club   1955–57
7300 Woodrow Wilson Dr.
Los Angeles, CA 90046
Chapter #90, Classic Thunderbird Club International

COLORADO

Colorado Classic Thunderbird Club   1955–57
P.O. Box 1343
Arvada, Colorado 80001
Chapter 6, Classic Thunderbird Club International

Rocky Mountain Thunderbird Club   All years
P. O. Box 12281
Aurora, CO 80012

CONNECTICUT

Connecticut Area Classic Thunderbird Club   1955–57
30 Whiting Street
Willimantic, CT 06226-3328
Chapter #44, Classic Thunderbird Club International

FLORIDA

Central Florida Classic Thunderbirds   1955–57
6625 Crenshaw Dr.
Orlando, FL 32835
Chapter #67, Classic Thunderbird Club International

Sunbirds of Florida, Inc   1955–57
1501 Grandview Dr.
Tapron Springs, FL 34689
Chapter #29, Classic Thunderbird Club International

GEORGIA

North Georgia Vintage Thunderbird Club   1958–97
104 Paddock Trail
Peachtree City, GA 30269
Affiliated with Vintage Thunderbird Club International

HAWAII

Classic Birds of Paradise   1955–57
558 Palawiki St.
Kailua, HI 96734-3502
Affiliated with the Classic Thunderbird Club International

IDAHO

Idaho Vintage Thunderbird Club   1958–69
11115 Gunsmoke
Boise ID 83713
Affiliated with Heartland Vintage Thunderbird Club of America

ILLINOIS

Chicagoland Thunderbirds   All years
107A S. Highland Ave.
Lombard, IL 60148
Affiliated with Vintage Thunderbird Club International

Classic Thunderbird Club of Chicagoland   1955–57
995 Auburn Lane
Bartlett, IL 60103
Chapter #9, Classic Thunderbird Club International

INDIANA

Vintage Thunderbird Club of Indiana   1958–97
8575 N. County Rd.
650 E. Brownsburg, IN. 46112
Chapter of Vintage Thunderbird Club International

KANSAS

Wichita Classic Thunderbird Club   1955–57
355 N. Hillside
Wichita, KS. 67214
Chapter #16, Classic Thunderbird Club International

LOUISIANA

Acadian Thunderbird Club, Inc   All years
1605 Nie Parkway
New Orleans LA 70131
Affiliated with Vintage Thunderbird Club International

MARYLAND

Potomac Classic Thunderbird Club   1955–57
5231 Ilex Way
Dayton, MD 21036
Chapter #23, Classic Thunderbird Club International

MASSACHUSETTS

Classic Thunderbirds of New England   1955–57
P.O. Box 342
Lynnfield, MA. 01940
Chapter #11, Classic Thunderbird Club International

Thunderbirds of Western New England   1955–57
200 Shaker Road
East Longmeadow MA 01028
Chapter #111, Classic Thunderbird Club International

T-BIRD CLUBS

MICHIGAN

The American Road Thunderbird Club   1955–57
P.O. Box 1221
Dearborn, MI 48121
Chapter #5, Classic Thunderbird Club International

Water Wonderland Thunderbird Club   1955–71
3832 Nash
Troy, MI 48083
Affiliated with Vintage Thunderbird Club International

MINNESOTA

Mini-Birds of Minnesota   1955–57
1117 W. Wayzata Blvd.
Long Lake, MN
Chapter #32, Classic Thunderbird Club International

Thunderbird Midwest   1958–97
4380 245th St
Forest Lake, MN 55025-9046
Affiliated with Vintage Thunderbird Club International

MISSOURI

Vintage Thunderbirds of Kansas City   1958–97
609 E. 72nd ST
Kansas City MO 64131-1613
Affiliated with Vintage Thunderbird Club International

NEBRASKA

Classic Thunderbird Club of Omaha   1958–97
1251 Reece Rd.
Goddard, KS 67052-9330
Chapter of Vintage Thunderbird Club International

Nebraskaland Thunderbird Club   1955–57
8721 Pratt
Omaha NE 68134
Chapter #65, Classic Thunderbird Club International

NEW JERSEY

Garden State Late 'Birds, Inc   All years
22 Hoffman Drive
Hamilton Square, NJ 08690
*Affiliated with Heartland Vintage Thunderbird Club,
Vintage Thunderbird, Club International, International
Thunderbird Club*

New Jersey Open Road Thunderbird Club   1955–57
P.O. Box 565
Hewitt, NJ 07421
Chapter #41, Classic Thunderbird Club International

NEW MEXICO

Clovis Thunderbirds   1960–64
1800 Mitchell
Clovis NM

Pajarito Thunderbird Club of New Mexico   1955–57
2800 Calle Grande N.W.
Albuquerque NM 87104
Affiliated with Classic Thunderbird Club International

NEW YORK

Buffalo Thunderbird Club   All years
S. 5845 Ainslee Lane
Lakeview, NY 14085
*Affiliated with Classic Thunderbird Club International
and Vintage Thunderbird Club International*

Classic Thunderbirds of the Hudson Valley   1955–57
90 Jack and Jill Road
Poughquag, NY 12570
Affiliated with Classic Thunderbird Club International

Thunderbird Owners of New York   1955–57
56 Park Circle South
Farmingdale, NY 11735
Affiliated with Classic Thunderbird Club International

Upstate New York Thunderbird Club, Inc   All years
401 Peck Rd #25
Kirkville NY 13082
Affiliated with International Thunderbird Club

OHIO

Classic Thunderbird Club of Northern Ohio   1955–57
465 Michael
N. Olmstead, OH 44070-2916
Chapter #2, Classic Thunderbird Club International

Heartland-Ohio Vintage Thunderbird Club   1958–69
6700 Spokane Dr
Huber Heights, OH 45424
Affiliated with Heartland Vintage Thunderbird Club of America

The Maumee Valley Thunderbirds   1955–57
5861 Globe Ave
Toledo, OH 43615
Chapter #70, Classic Thunderbird Club International

Ohio Valley Early Birds, Inc   1955–57
P.O. Box 24583
Huber Heights, OH 45424
Chapter #68, Classic Thunderbird Club International

OKLAHOMA

Lawton Lil' Birds   1955–57
1001 NW 16th
Lawton, Ok 73507
Chapter #105, Classic Thunderbird Club International

Tulsa Classic Thunderbird Club   1955–57
3733 E. 31st Street
Tulsa, OK 74135-1506
Chapter #7, Classic Thunderbird Club International

PENNSYLVANIA

Lehigh Valley Thunderbird Club, Inc   All years
P O Box 21973, Lehigh Valley PA 18002-1973
*Affiliated with International Thunderbird Club and
Classic Thunderbird Club International*

North East Thunderbirds   All years
539 21st Ave.
Altoona, PA 16601

RHODE ISLAND

South Shores Thunderbirds   All years
81 Lawn St.
Providence, RI, 02908-4042
Affiliated with Vintage Thunderbird Club International

TEXAS

Big "D" Little Birds   1955–57
P.O. Box 835052
Richardson,TX 75083
Chapter #46, Classic Thunderbird Club International

Capitol City Thunderbird Club   1958–66
8200 Pitter Pat Lane
Austin, Texas 78736
Chapter of Vintage Thunderbird Club International

Classic Thunderbirds of Houston   1955–57
P.O. Box 1478
Bellaire, TX 77402-1478
Chapter #34, Classic Thunderbird Club

Metroplex Early Birds   1955–57
10103 Candlebrook Dr.
Dallas, TX 75243
Chapter #26, Classic Thunderbird Club International

North Texas Vintage Thunderbirds   1958–96
P.O. Box 988
Wylie TX 75098
Chapter of Vintage Thunderbird Club International

San Antonio Classic Thunderbird Club   1955–57
2318 Estate Gate Drive
San Antonio, TX 78250
Chapter #20, Classic Thunderbird Club International

South Texas Thunderbird Club   All years
1161 Galway Gate
Canyon Lake, TX 78133-3007
Affiliated with Vintage Thunderbird Club International

UTAH

Open Road T-Bird Club   1955–57
1402 East Maple Hills Drive
Bountiful, Utah 84010

VIRGINIA

Blue Ridge Classic Thunderbird Club   1955–57
130 Longcroft Rd.
Winchester, VA 22602
Chapter #82, Classic Thunderbird Club International

Virginia Classic Thunderbird Club, Inc   1955–57
311 Farnham Drive
Richmond, VA 23236
Chapter #36, Classic Thunderbird Club International

WASHINGTON

Olympic Thunderbird Club   1955–57
5516 3rd Ave. So.
Seattle, WA 98108
Chapter #1, Classic Thunderbird Club International

T-BIRD CLUBS

Pacific Northwest Chapter   1958–66
13030–7th Avenue South
Seattle, Washington 98168-2710
Chapter of Vintage Thunderbird Club International

WISCONSIN

Classic Thunderbird Club of Wisconsin   1955–69
866 So. 75th Street
West Allis, WI 53214-3013
*Affiliated with Classic Thunderbird Club International,
Vintage Thunderbird Club International, International
Thunderbird Club*

AUSTRALIA
QUEENSLAND

Thunderbirds of Queensland Inc.   All years
10 Mako Avenue
Birkdale, Queensland, 4159

SOUTH AUSTRALIA

Thunderbird Owners Club of Australia Inc.   All years
6 Koonya Ave.
Seaford, 5169 South Australia

BRAZIL

Watanabe's T-bird Club   All years
rua Sir Winston Churchill, #110
Cravinhos, Sao Paulo
14140-000 Brazil

CANADA
BRITISH COLUMBIA

Island Vintage Thunderbird Club   1955–66
2294 Greenlands Road
Victoria, B.C.
Canada V8N 4T4

Totem Thunderbird Club of British Columbia
     All years
c/o 2676-167 St.
South Surrey, B.C.
Canada, V4B 5E7
*Chapter #80, Classic Thunderbird Club International and
affiliated with Vintage Thunderbird Club International*

ONTARIO

Southern Ontario Thunderbird Club   All years
2580 Robin Drive
Mississauga, Ontario
Canada L5K 2H9

NEW ZEALAND

Ford Thunderbird Owners Club of New Zealand Inc.
     1955–1997
12 Highfield Cres.
Tauranga, New Zealand.

*Listings courtesy of Jerry Wotel of The Thunderbird
Cybernest (http://www.tbird.org/tcn.shtml).*

PHOTOGRAPHY CREDITS

Archive Photos:
pp. 73, 94, 97, 103

Automobile Quarterly Publications:
pp. 9, 16-17, 25, 26-27 both, 28, 29, 30-31, 32, 33, 34-35, 36-37 top,
41 both, 42-43 top, 45 both, 46-47, 48-49 both, 50-51, 56, 62-63,
64-65, 68, 74-75, 78-79, 80-81 both, 82-83 both, 98-99, 100-101

Corbis-Bettmann:
p. 105

Duke University Libraries/J. Walter Thompson Collection:
pp. 44, 53, 58, 76

©Jay Hirsch:
pp. 60-61

©Ron Kimball:
pp. 2, 8, 10-11, 13, 15 top, 18-19, 86, 88-89, 95

Daniel B. Lyons Collection:
p. 115

©Doug Mitchell:
p. 40

©Mike Mueller:
pp. 5, 7, 14, 15 bottom, 20-21, 22, 37 bottom, 38-39 both,
70-71 both, 106-107 both, 110-111, 112, 113, 114

Mike Mueller Collection:
p. 102

©Steve Swope:
pp. 108-109

©National Motor Museum/Nicky Wright:
p. 43 bottom

UPI/Corbis-Bettmann:
pp. 12, 23

George Watts Collection:
pp. 52, 54, 59, 66-67, 77, 84-85

©Nicky Wright:
pp. 24, 90, 92-93, 96

©Superstock:
endpapers

INDEX